The never-ending story of how to feed a family . . .

how to feed a family

THE SWEET POTATO CHRONICLES COOKBOOK

LAURA KEOGH & CERI MARSH · photography by MAYA VISNYEI

appetite
by RANDOM HOUSE

Appetite by Random House and colophon are registered trademarks of Random House of Canada Limited

Library and Archives of Canada Cataloguing in Publication is available upon request

ISBN: 978-0-449-01573-5

Editor: Martha Kanya-Forstner
Cover and book design: CS Richardson
Food stylist and recipe developer: Heather Shaw
Prop stylist: Catherine Doherty

PRINTED AND BOUND IN CHINA

Published in Canada by Appetite by Random House,
a division of Random House of Canada Limited

www.randomhouse.ca

10 9 8 7 6 5 4 3 2

Julian, Esme and Scarlett—
this book is for you and because of you.

Contents

Introduction

O F THE THOUSANDS OF THINGS that change when you have kids, food has to top the list. It certainly did for us. As long-time editors at a fashion magazine we had plenty of opportunities to report on health and nutrition. We were aware of processed food traps, knew about the benefits of organic produce and meats and understood that sugar was nobody's friend. We both enjoyed cooking and, for the most part, maintained healthy diets. However, we also inhabited a world where three hors d'oeuvres and a glass of champagne often constituted dinner. So it was a world-rocking shift to suddenly have children who needed to be fed—regularly. By the time our kids reached the solid food milestone the enormity of the task had begun to sink in. They need another meal? And another? And *another*? We were overwhelmed not just with the relentlessness of the cooking, but the responsibility it represented. It was one thing to have a casual relationship with nutrition for ourselves, but when we were feeding our babies? That was a whole new ballgame. It became clear to us that we needed an approach to this madness or we'd be found listless, spirit-broken at the bottom of a box of snack crackers.

And so we started our website, Sweet Potato Chronicles (www. sweetpotatochronicles.com). Our motivations were largely selfish. We wanted a place where we could figure out this family food business, share our findings about health and nutrition and be connected to like-minded parents. Because we're journalists we took on the task of learning how to keep our families healthy the same way we would any other assignment. We love sharing our research, whether it's a recipe for a low-sugar after-school snack or the latest thinking on vitamin D levels. We're not chefs. In fact, we're far from it. We're parents who are trying to find the balance between doing the best we can for our families and maintaining some sanity. This book is the result of all that thinking and cooking and blogging. It reflects what we care about and what we think can really make a difference. These are not hard-and-fast rules. We try to keep the pressure off. After all, the last thing you need is more to feel guilty about. Here are a few things we've figured out, and we hope they will be useful for your family, too.

✳ **If you're eating at home, half the nutrition battle is won.** Of course, there are those days when the only thing keeping you going is knowing that the local pizza joint is cooking tonight's dinner. And to that we say, "Hell, yes." But chances are the food you prepare for your family is going to be far healthier than anything they can order off a menu. Committing to making most of the food your family eats is, in our opinion, the biggest step you can take toward overall health.

✳ **Put kids in touch with food.** Literally. We may daydream about a garden where we grow all our own produce but the reality is that we're urban parents. So, we take the kids to the local farmers' market and get them planting basil on the deck. Even more important is that we get the kids cooking with us once the food comes home. We know, we know: the mess. But the investment you make in time and mess will pay dividends when you see your kid full of pride, tucking into a healthy and delicious (remember, none of this means anything if we forget food should be yummy) dish they helped prepare.

Be flexible. Actually, be flexitarian. We're not vegetarians but we believe in making at least one or two meatless dinners each week. The health benefits are proven to be significant, plus we like establishing that a meal doesn't have to be "a meat and two veg" to be legit.

 Back away from the sugar. We know that obesity and its long-term consequences are among the most pressing health issues facing children today. We believe that treats should be just that—a treat, not for every day. Of course, there's a time and place for dessert, and we'll be the first to help ourselves, thank you very much! But if you don't establish what the basic rules on treats are going to be for your family (dessert once a week? modest portions?), the world is going to do it for you. And rest assured, you are not the meanest parent in the world if you sometimes say no to the endless goodie-train.

 How do we navigate the grocery store? In a perfect world we'd feed our kids foods cultivated by angels, free from antibiotics and pesticides, and damn the expense. In reality it's not so simple to control the provenance of everything our kids consume. We all have to decide for ourselves where the line is. We prefer meat to be organic and would rather eat less of it in order to rationalize the expense. We also like to eat seasonally when we can since certain foods, especially berries, apples and vegetables, are less expensive when they haven't been trucked in from Timbuktu. And even though we grew up on peanut butter and jelly sandwiches made with fluffy white bread (mmmmm!), we're of the mind that it's best to use whole grains in everything from bread to rice to pasta. You'll notice we don't specify what kind of milk, yogurt or butter to use in most recipes and that's by design. We've created these recipes so you can use what you've got—2% or soy milk, salted or unsalted butter. After all, we don't want anything to stand in the way of you trying them. We've also included some ingredients we love, like chia and agave nectar, but they can be hard to find. Don't worry, they are either optional or we've offered readily available alternatives.

❋ **We're late. All the time. Aren't you?** And that's why you're not going to find a lot of overly complicated recipes here. We like recipes that work within the framework of real households. You won't find 60 steps to a bouillabaisse—not because we don't love bouillabaisse, but because we don't have the time for it. Most of our recipes can come together in the time you have between getting home from piano lessons and a hunger-induced meltdown—so what's that?—about 45 minutes?

❋ **Rather than give you a play-by-play of the nutritional breakdown of every recipe, we decided to give you highlights throughout the book.** We prefer—as do a lot of nutrition experts—to think of nutrition over the course of a day or even a week rather than to obsess over every meal and snack. Keep an eye out for our What's So Great About? sidebars that will pop up throughout the book when we're particularly excited about an ingredient.

❋ As you cook your way through this book, you will see these symbols to help you spot key features of a recipe at a glance:

This						1 MONDAY
Means This	meatless	kids can help	fast	minimal mess	entertaining	make ahead

But let's face it, feeding a family is as much an art as it is a science, and there is so much more to food than . . . well, food. We're also sharing some of the strategies that have worked in our own families when it comes to hot topics like pickiness, manners and chores. We hope you'll feel encouraged to get in the kitchen and have fun. And know that despite your best efforts sometimes it all goes terribly wrong: something burns, everything spills, nobody likes it. We've all been there. Just remember, for better or worse, there's always another day, and another chapter in the never-ending story of how to feed a family. LK & CM

WEEKDAY BREAKFAST

Toad-in-a-Hole

Apple Ginger Milkshake

Berry Blaster Smoothie

Funky Monkey Shake

Maya's Morning Wake-up Call

Breakfast Cookie

Sweet Potato French Toast

Pumpkin Granola

Zoë's Bakery Cafe's Famous Muesli

Slow Cooker Oatmeal with Coconut, Banana and Almonds

Oatmeal and Strawberry Blender Pancakes

Baked Spiced Apple and Sweet Potato Toaster Tarts

Strawberry, Ricotta and Mint Breakfast Quesadilla

WEEKEND BREAKFAST

Whole Wheat Pancakes

Peanut Butter Pancakes with Jelly Syrup

Lemony Yogurt Pancakes with Blueberry Syrup

Egg Bakes

Tortilla Scramble

Baked French Toast with Crumble Topping

Biscuits Two Ways

BRUNCH PARTY

Pomegranate Rosemary Cocktail

Simple Prosciutto Strata

Fennel Citrus Salad

Sweet Potato Hash Browns

Plum and Peach German Pancake

Toad-in-a-Hole

A s a child, my husband, Dan, enjoyed the traditional English dish of
sausage in a Yorkshire pudding batter. In its North American incarnation
Toad-in-a-Hole is an easy egg breakfast. The dish lends itself to a lot of
variations that increase its nutritional punch. This one pairs our toad with an apple
and cheddar slaw. Sprinkle the slaw overtop the warm, right-out-of-the-pan egg.
You could also try shredded ham, avocado, grated pear, grated carrot or even a slice
of tofu instead of the slaw. Dan cringed at the thought of tofu on his beloved toad,
but you can't trust the opinion of a man who puts hot dogs in his mac and cheese.
Or can you? LK

Prep time: 5 minutes
Total time: 30 minutes
Makes: 2 servings

2 Tbsp (30 ml) unsalted butter
1 Granny Smith apple
¼ cup (60 ml) shredded cheddar cheese
4 slices spelt bread
4 eggs

In a large frying pan over medium-low heat,
melt 1 Tbsp (15 ml) of the butter.

While the butter is melting, chop or use a mandolin to slice
the apple and cheddar into matchstick-size pieces. Set aside.
Using a cookie cutter or a glass, cut holes in the center of
each bread slice.

Place two slices of bread in the frying pan and allow to
lightly brown on one side, about 2 minutes. Flip the bread
over and crack an egg into each hole. Allow the eggs to cook
through, about 6 minutes. Remove and sprinkle with the
slaw or serve the slaw as a side. Repeat with the remaining
butter, bread and eggs.

Apple Ginger Milkshake

Berry Blaster Smoothie

Funky Monkey Shake

Maya's Morning Wake-Up Call

See overleaf for recipes

Apple Ginger Milkshake

THIS LITTLE APPLE DITTY gets its rich flavor from the addition of pumpkin butter, and it offers the anti-inflammatory benefits of fresh ginger. I like to think of it as a prescription rather than a treat. LK

Prep time: 5 minutes
Total time: 7 minutes
Makes: 2 servings

1 ½ cups (375 ml) milk
¾ cup (185 ml) Greek yogurt
1 Tbsp (15 ml) pumpkin butter
    (or almond or peanut butter)
1 Gala apple, cored and sliced
1 tsp (5 ml) maple syrup
½ tsp (2 ml) grated fresh ginger

Place the milk, yogurt, pumpkin butter, apple slices and maple syrup in a blender and pulse until the apple is finely minced. Add the ginger and pulse until incorporated. Pour and serve.

Berry Blaster Smoothie

WE ALWAYS KEEP frozen berries in the freezer so we can whip up this smoothie any time. The combination of berries, pomegranate and high-protein Greek yogurt gives it an immunity-boosting shot. CM

Prep time: 3 minutes
Total time: 5 minutes
Makes: 2 servings

2 cups (500 ml) frozen mixed berries
1 cup (250 ml) Greek yogurt
1 cup (250 ml) pomegranate juice
1 Tbsp (15 ml) honey

Toss all the ingredients into a blender and blend. You may need a bit more juice depending on how thick you like your smoothies. Pour and serve.

Funky Monkey Shake

TOSSING A COUPLE of bananas in the freezer the night before makes all the difference to this shake. Your kids might even think you were sleepy enough to use ice cream. CM

Prep time: 5 minutes
Total time: 7 minutes
Makes: 2 servings

2 frozen bananas, peeled and chopped

2 cups (500 ml) milk or soy milk

2 Tbsp (30 ml) smooth natural almond
    or peanut butter

1 Tbsp (15 ml) maple syrup

1 Tbsp (15 ml) flax meal

½ cup (125 ml) Greek yogurt

Get everything into the blender and give it a whiz. Pour and serve.

Maya's Morning Wake-Up Call

MAYA VISNYEI, the woman responsible for all the gorgeous photographs in this book, is calm, beautiful and fearless (ever try taking a picture of a kid who is not only having a meltdown but who also happens to be holding a rolling pin?). This—the smoothie of champions—is what Maya throws back before a long day of shooting with us. LK

Prep time: 5 minutes
Total time: 7 minutes
Makes: 2 servings

1 orange, peeled and sliced

1 banana, peeled and halved

1 cup (250 ml) carrot juice

Put the orange slices, banana halves and carrot juice in a blender and pulse until blended. Serve immediately.

Breakfast Cookie

MADE THESE IN AN EFFORT to create the cookie version of one of my daughter, Esme's, obsessions: toasted almond butter and banana sandwiches. Serve these cookies with some fresh fruit and a little yogurt. If you're really pressed for time, pop them in a lunch bag, to be eaten on the go. CM

Prep time: 10 minutes
Total time: 25 minutes
Makes: 10 big cookies

1 really ripe banana

1 egg

½ cup (125 ml) natural almond
    or peanut butter

⅓ cup (80 ml) maple syrup

½ tsp (2 ml) vanilla extract

1 cup (250 ml) spelt flour

1 cup (250 ml) old-fashioned oats

½ cup (125 ml) shredded
    unsweetened coconut

¼ cup (60 ml) flax meal

½ tsp (2 ml) baking powder

¼ tsp (1 ml) baking soda

Preheat the oven to 375°F (190°C). Line two baking sheets with parchment paper.

In a large mixing bowl, mash up your banana, then add the egg, nut butter, syrup and vanilla. Use an electric mixer to blend it all together.

In a second bowl, combine the flour, oats, coconut, flax, baking powder and baking soda. Add the wet ingredients to the dry in three additions, mixing well between each addition.

Using a ½ cup (125 ml) measure, scoop the batter onto the prepared baking sheets, leaving about 2 inches (5 cm) between the cookies. Bake for 12 to 14 minutes, until the cookies are golden brown. Give them a couple of minutes on your counter before transferring them to a rack to cool completely.

, too big

WHAT'S SO GREAT ABOUT SPELT? Spelt is considered an ancient grain. Its recent popularity is due to the fact that it has a broader spectrum of nutrients like protein, copper and zinc than its more manufactured friend wheat. It also plays nice with the bellies of folks who are intolerant of wheat. LK

Sweet Potato French Toast

CAN THROW DOWN THIS DISH faster than my daughter, Scarlett, can say, "Can I have cereal instead?" Combine the protein from the eggs, the vitamin A–rich sweet potato, whole grains (you promise to use whole grains, right?) and the anti-inflammatory cinnamon dressing, and you've got yourself a breakfast that will fire the brain for a busy day. Ask that colorful box of cereal on the table if it can do all that. LK

Prep time: 10 minutes
Total time: 20 minutes
Makes: 2 servings

2 Tbsp (30 ml) unsalted butter
4 slices spelt bread
¼ cup (60 ml) sweet potato purée
    (recipe below)
2 eggs
½ cup (125 ml) milk
1 tsp (5 ml) maple syrup or agave nectar
¼ tsp (1 ml) ground cinnamon
Ground nutmeg
Maple syrup or agave nectar for drizzling

Melt 1 Tbsp (15 ml) of the butter in a frying pan over medium heat. Cut each slice of bread into four lengthwise sticks.

Whisk the sweet potato purée with the eggs, milk and agave nectar. Add the cinnamon and a pinch of nutmeg. Sink each stick from two slices of bread in the egg mixture and flip to coat completely. Place the egg-soaked bread 8 sticks at a time into the hot pan.

Cook for 3 minutes and then flip. Cook for another 2 minutes and remove from the pan. Add the remaining 1 Tbsp (15 ml) of butter to the pan and cook the remaining sticks of bread. Stack and serve warm with maple syrup or agave nectar.

Sweet Potato or Pumpkin Purée

A large sweet potato or small sugar pumpkin (don't go for the big Jack-O'-Lantern fellows) will yield more purée than you'll need for any given recipe but it freezes well. For easy usage, I like to freeze ¼ cup (60 ml) amounts in small, well-sealed freezer bags. You can either boil or roast sweet potatoes or sugar pumpkins. Boiling is quicker but roasting results in a better flavor.

To boil: peel and cut your veg into 2-inch (5 cm) chunks. Toss them in a large pot of boiling water and simmer until tender, 10 to 15 minutes.

Remove from the heat and drain. Using a handheld potato masher and large bowl, or a food processor, mash until smooth.

To bake: preheat the oven to 400°F (200°C). Pierce the sweet potatoes with a fork and wrap in aluminum foil. Slice the sugar pumpkin into quarters and spoon out the guts. Place the veggies on a baking sheet and bake for 30 to 40 minutes. Check that they're fork-tender. Remove from the oven, and allow to cool slightly before scooping out the flesh and mashing or puréeing until smooth. CM

Pumpkin Granola

S O MANY STORE-BOUGHT granolas are packed with oil and sugar that it's nice to whip up a batch of your own when you have the time. It's worth the effort to hunt down brown rice syrup at the grocery store, as it's far lower on the glycemic index than corn syrup (which you'd use otherwise). My son, Julian, is a cereal fiend and has been known to put away three bowls of this before starting his day. CM

Prep time: 15 minutes
Total time: 40 minutes
Makes: 10 ½-cup (125 ml) servings

½ cup (125 ml) oats
½ cup (125 ml) finely chopped almonds
½ cup (125 ml) finely chopped pecans
½ cup (125 ml) finely chopped
    pumpkin seeds
½ cup (125 ml) dried cranberries
¼ cup (60 ml) shredded
    unsweetened coconut
¼ cup (60 ml) wheat germ
¼ cup (60 ml) flax meal
½ tsp (2 ml) ground cinnamon
¼ cup (60 ml) brown rice syrup
1 Tbsp (15 ml) maple syrup
1 Tbsp (15 ml) vegetable oil
½ cup (125 ml) pumpkin purée
    (see page 17)

Preheat the oven to 350°F (180°C). Line a baking sheet with parchment paper.

In a large bowl, toss together the oats, almonds, pecans, pumpkin seeds, cranberries, coconut, wheat germ, flax meal and cinnamon.

In another bowl, mix together the syrups, oil and pumpkin purée. Pour this wet mixture over the dry and combine well. It will be sticky!

Spread the mixture over the prepared baking sheet. Press it down with the back of a spoon until it's about ½ inch (1 cm) thick. Bake for 20 to 25 minutes until the edges are starting to turn brown. The granola will firm up as it cools, so don't worry if the center is still soft.

Cool the granola completely before breaking it into small chunks. Store in an airtight container in a cool, dry place for up to 2 weeks. Serve with milk, and fresh berries if you're feeling fancy.

Zoë's Bakery Cafe's Famous Muesli

S CARLETT AND I spend our Saturday mornings sharing a bowl of muesli at Zoë's Bakery Café in downtown Toronto. Chef Andrea Kennedy mixes apples, oranges, raisins and other dried fruits with toasted oats, yogurt and milk in a combination I have yet to replicate. Until now. Zoë's owner, Shawn Zolberg, has graciously agreed to unlock the secret of this antioxidant-rich morning dish for the benefit of this book. However, you'll still find me at Zoë's. After all these years, it's not just a neighborhood café, it's like the home of an old friend. LK

Prep time: 15 minutes
Total time: 20 minutes
Makes: 4 servings

2 cups (500 ml) rolled oats
½ cup (125 ml) slivered almonds
2-3 cups (500-750 ml) plain yogurt,
 plus extra for desired consistency
½ cup (125 ml) honey
½ cup (125 ml) milk, plus extra for
 desired consistency
½ tsp (2 ml) ground cinnamon
2 Granny Smith apples, diced
2 seedless oranges, diced
½ cup (125 ml) dried apricots, sliced
½ cup (125 ml) dried cranberries
¼ cup (60 ml) golden raisins (optional)

Preheat the oven to 350°F (180°C).

Spread the oats and slivered almonds on a baking sheet and toast until golden brown, 7 to 10 minutes. Remove from the oven and allow to cool.

Place the toasted oats and almonds in a large bowl and add the yogurt, honey, milk and cinnamon. Add the apple pieces, then orange pieces, followed by the apricots, cranberries, raisins, mixing after each addition.

Add more milk for desired thickness. Serve.

WHAT'S SO GREAT ABOUT APPLES? Although many of the health benefits of an apple are found in its peel, the sweet, crisp insides are also effective in moderating blood sugars, lowering cholesterol levels and boosting immune functions. CM

Slow Cooker Oatmeal
with Coconut, Banana and Almonds

M Y SLOW COOKER used to live in my appliance blind spot. That is, until I was introduced to this life-saving morning recipe. What better reason to start dating your slow cooker again than the ease of waking up to a warm pot of oatmeal? The coconut and almond milks give these oats a creamy texture and the flavor trifecta of caramelized brown sugar, bananas and cinnamon is sweetly satisfying. In other words, oatmeal ecstasy. LK

Prep time: 10 minutes

Total time: 8 hours 10 minutes

Makes: 4 servings

2 bananas

1 ¼ cups (310 ml) steel-cut oats

1 can (15 oz/443 ml) light coconut milk

1 ½ cups (375 ml) almond milk

¾ cup (185 ml) water

2 Tbsp (30 ml) coconut sugar
    or brown sugar

1 Tbsp (15 ml) ground white chia seeds
    (optional)

1 tsp (5 ml) vanilla extract

1 tsp (5 ml) ground cinnamon

½ tsp (2 ml) ground ginger

Salt

¼ cup (60 ml) whole almonds

shredded unsweetened coconut
    for garnish

Slice one of the bananas. Combine the banana slices, oats, coconut and almond milks, water, sugar, chia seeds, vanilla, cinnamon, ginger and salt in a slow cooker. Give it all a stir. Cook on low for 8 hours.

Serve topped with freshly sliced banana, almonds and shredded coconut.

WHAT'S SO GREAT ABOUT OATS?

Oatmeal and oat bran are a super source of both insoluble (absorbs water for healthy digestion) and soluble (easily digested) fiber. Oats pack cholesterol-lowering antioxidants as well as phytochemicals (plant chemicals) that may reduce the risk of some cancers. Oats also boast an impressive lineup of amino acids, essential proteins that help the body function at an optimum level, so you might want to toss them into just about everything. Use rolled, steel-cut or old–fashioned oats to reap the grain's goodness. LK

Oatmeal and Strawberry Blender Pancakes

THIS IS THE BUSY PARENT'S answer to pancakes. We promise they cook up fast and easy so you can get out the door on time. If they don't, Ceri will clean your kitchen. (She hates when I promise that!) LK

Prep time: 10 minutes
Total time: 20 minutes
Makes: 2 servings

1 ½ cups (375 ml) rolled multigrain oats
¾ cup (185 ml) milk
¼ cup (60 ml) Greek yogurt
1 ½ Tbsp (22 ml) strawberry or
   blueberry preserve
½ tsp (2 ml) vanilla extract
2 Tbsp (30 ml) unsalted butter
Agave nectar or maple syrup for drizzling

Place the oats, milk, yogurt, preserve and vanilla in a blender. Blend until smooth.

In a large frying pan over medium heat, melt 1 Tbsp (15 ml) of the butter. Drop 2 Tbsp (30 ml) of batter into the hot pan to form a pancake. Make three or four pancakes depending on the size of pan. Cook until bubbles form around the edges, 3 to 4 minutes, then flip. Cook for another minute and then remove them from the pan. Add the remaining 1 Tbsp (15 ml) of butter and then repeat with the remaining batter.

Serve the pancakes warm with agave nectar or maple syrup drizzled overtop.

Baked Spiced Apple and Sweet Potato Toaster Tarts

THERE IS NOTHING EASIER than grabbing something from the refrigerator, throwing it in the toaster oven and then handing it over to your dawdling daughter. (Why do they always dawdle?) If you reserve a Sunday to bake these toaster treats then you're guaranteed a week off from breakfast duty. What's that? The sound of you setting your alarm a little later? **LK**

Prep time: 45 minutes
Total time: 1 hour 10 minutes
Makes: 5 tarts

Pastry

2 cups (500 ml) spelt flour
2 Tbsp (30 ml) brown sugar
1 tsp (5 ml) salt
1 tsp (5 ml) ground cinnamon
1 cup (250 ml) cold unsalted butter, grated
1 large egg
2 Tbsp (30 ml) milk

Filling

1 sweet potato
1 tsp (5 ml) vanilla extract
¼ tsp (1 ml) ground ginger
1 apple, peeled, cored and cut into
    1-inch (2.5 cm) or smaller pieces
1 Tbsp (15 ml) fresh lemon juice
2 tsp (10 ml) butter
1 Tbsp (15 ml) brown sugar
1 Tbsp (15 ml) maple syrup
1 egg

Glaze (optional)

½ cup (125 ml) sifted confectioners' sugar
¼ tsp (1 ml) ground cinnamon
1 Tbsp (15 ml) milk
1 tsp (5 ml) vanilla extract

See overleaf for preparation

Line a baking sheet with parchment paper.

For the pastry, whisk together the flour, brown sugar, salt and cinnamon. Add the butter 1 Tbsp (15 ml) at a time and mix well. Beat the egg with the milk in a separate bowl and then add to the flour mixture. Mix until completely combined and then form into a ball, wrap in plastic wrap and place in the refrigerator while you prepare the filling.

For the filling, peel the sweet potato and cut it into even-sized pieces. Boil them until cooked, about 15 minutes. Cool. Place in a food processor with the vanilla and ginger and pulse until smooth. Refrigerate until needed.

Toss the apple pieces with the lemon juice in a bowl. In a medium-sized saucepan, melt the butter over medium-low heat until it begins to brown lightly. Add the apple, brown sugar and maple syrup and cook until the apple is soft but crisp, 8 to 10 minutes.

Remove the apple from the heat and allow to cool. Refrigerate while you work on the pastry.

Remove the pastry dough from the refrigerator. Roll out the dough on a floured surface until it is ⅛ inch (2 mm) thick. Cut it into 10 even-sized rectangles. Place half the rectangles on the prepared baking sheet and refrigerate while you work with the other rectangles.

Remove the sweet potato and apple mixtures from the refrigerator and blend them together. (You may want to remove some of the liquid from the apple. The mixture should not be runny.)

Beat the egg and brush each of the dough pieces with it. Place a heaping Tbsp (25 ml) of the filling in the center of each rectangle and flatten it with the back of a spoon. Remove the reserved dough from the refrigerator and use it to top the filled rectangles. Press the floured tines of a fork along the edges of the pastry to close the two halves, then press into the center to create a vent.

Preheat the oven to 350°F (180°C). Bake the tarts in the oven for 20 minutes, or until golden brown. Allow to cool on a baking rack.

For the glaze, in a medium-sized bowl, whisk the sifted confectioners' sugar with the cinnamon. Add the milk and vanilla and mix well. Using a fork, drizzle the glaze in a criss-cross pattern overtop the tarts.

Store in an airtight container (with parchment between tarts if you have glazed them) in the refrigerator for up to 1 week.

Strawberry, Ricotta and Mint Breakfast Quesadilla

LOVE MEXICAN CUISINE and can be conned into most anything with the promise of a burrito. This recipe is my dinner addiction brought to life as a breakfast. The combination of sweet cheese, strawberries and mint in all its oozy glory is only made better by a drizzle of maple syrup. Assembly is fast and easy, so if you mix up the cheese and berries the night before, you can get these on the breakfast table in minutes. Pinky swear. **LK**

Prep time: 10 minutes
Total time: 25 minutes
Makes: 4 servings

1 ½ cups (375 ml) ricotta cheese
½ cup (125 ml) cottage cheese
3 Tbsp (45 ml) sugar
1 tsp (5 ml) vanilla extract
1 tsp (5 ml) chopped mint,
    plus sprigs for garnish
Zest of 1 lemon
1 cup (250 ml) sliced strawberries,
    plus additional for serving
2 tsp (10 ml) butter
4 medium-size spelt tortillas
Maple syrup for serving

In a medium bowl, combine the ricotta and cottage cheeses with the sugar, vanilla, mint and lemon zest. Gently stir in 1 cup (250 ml) of sliced strawberries. (You can do this step the night before. Just cover the bowl and refrigerate.)

In a medium frying pan, melt ½ tsp (2 ml) of the butter over medium-low heat. Place a tortilla in the pan and lightly brown on both sides.

Spread ½ cup (125 ml) of the cheese mixture onto the tortilla in the pan. Cook for 1 minute and then fold the tortilla in half. Allow to cook for another 2 minutes. Remove from the pan and repeat with the remaining tortillas.

Top with strawberries and mint and drizzle with maple syrup to serve.

Whole Wheat Pancakes

THERE WAS A TIME when we considered making pancakes the sole focus of the SPC website. Honestly. We're constantly trying different variations but every family needs a go-to classic. This recipe is it. The pancakes it delivers are fluffy, tender and, as a bonus, healthy. You could doll them up with berries or chocolate chips (hey, it's the weekend!) but all they need is a generous pour of maple syrup. Sometimes simple really is best. CM

Prep time: 10 minutes
Total time: 25 minutes
Makes: 10–12 4-inch (10 cm) pancakes

1 ½ cups (375 ml) whole wheat flour
2 tsp (10 ml) baking powder
¼ tsp (1 ml) salt
1 ½ cups (375 ml) milk
2 eggs
1 Tbsp (15 ml) butter (approximately)

Preheat the oven to 200°F (95°C). In a large bowl, combine the flour, baking powder and salt. In a smaller bowl, whisk together the milk and eggs. Pour the wet ingredients into the dry and mix until just combined. Don't overmix or your pancakes will be tough.

Melt about 1 tsp (5 ml) of the butter in a large frying pan over medium heat. Using a ¼ cup (60 ml) measure, ladle the batter into the warm pan. Once bubbles form around the edges of the pancakes, flip them over and cook on the other side, 2 or 3 minutes a side. Place the cooked pancakes on a plate and keep them in a warm oven as you keep working.

Serve with maple syrup and a smile.

Peanut Butter Pancakes
with Jelly Syrup

CAN REMEMBER BEING VERY SMALL, sitting around a big table enjoying pancakes with my entire family. My uncle always sold them as the *best* breakfast. I've since realized his claim was just a way of getting us all into the kitchen at the same time. After all, pancakes require constant attention and care, and no one wants to miss them when they're warm. These peanut butter cakes are lighter than you might expect, and the sweet jelly topping makes syrup unnecessary. I've tested this dish with my family of aficionados. The verdict? We loved them as much as we relished the morning we spent making them together. LK

Prep time: 10 minutes
Total time: 30 minutes
Makes: 4 servings

1 cup (250 ml) plain yogurt

½ cup (125 ml) buttermilk
(if you don't have any buttermilk, just add 1 ½ tsp/7.5 ml white vinegar to ½ cup/125 ml milk and let it stand for 10 minutes)

1 ½ tsp (7.5 ml) baking soda

1 ½ tsp (7.5 ml) baking powder

½ cup (125 ml) fresh fruit of choice

¼ cup (60 ml) fruit jelly

⅔ cup (160 ml) spelt flour

½ cup (125 ml) whole wheat flour

1 tsp (5 ml) chia powder (optional)

¼ tsp (1 ml) salt

1 cup (250 ml) smooth peanut butter

2 Tbsp (30 ml) agave nectar or maple syrup

2 large eggs, room temperature

2 Tbsp (30 ml) unsalted butter, room temperature (more if required)

Place the yogurt, buttermilk, baking soda and baking powder in a small bowl, stir to combine and set aside.

Put the fresh fruit and fruit jelly in a small food processor or blender and pulse until smooth. Set this fruit syrup aside in a small dish.

In a large bowl, place both flours, chia powder and salt, and whisk until incorporated.

Add the peanut butter, agave nectar and eggs to the yogurt mixture and whisk until smooth.

Slowly add the dry ingredients to the yogurt mixture. Stir gently until completely incorporated.

Heat a large griddle on medium heat and melt 1 tsp (5 ml) of the butter. Ladle ¼ cup (60 ml) of batter onto the griddle. Spread the batter into 4-inch (10 cm) circles and cook for 2 minutes on each side until golden brown, flipping only once. Using more butter as needed, repeat with the remaining batter.

Transfer the warm pancakes to plates, drizzle with fruit syrup and serve.

Lemony Yogurt Pancakes
with Blueberry Syrup

A BATCH OF THESE TENDER, very lemony lovelies is just the thing when you feel like something special. They're no more effort, just more heavenly than traditional pancakes. CM

Prep time: 10 minutes

Total time: 30 minutes

Makes: 12 smallish pancakes

2 eggs

1 cup (250 ml) Greek yogurt

¼ cup (60 ml) milk

3 Tbsp (45 ml) butter, melted

¼ cup (60 ml) fresh lemon juice

½ tsp (2 ml) lemon zest

½ tsp (2 ml) vanilla extract

1 cup (250 ml) spelt flour

¼ cup (60 ml) whole wheat flour

2 Tbsp (30 ml) sugar

1 Tbsp (15 ml) baking powder

1 tsp (5 ml) salt

Butter or vegetable oil for frying

Blueberry syrup (recipe page 36)

Preheat the oven to 200°F (95°C).

In a bowl, whisk together the eggs, yogurt, milk, melted butter, lemon juice and zest and vanilla. In another bowl, mix together both flours, the sugar, baking powder and salt.

Stir the wet ingredients into the dry until they are just combined. Never overmix pancakes. It makes them tough.

Heat a bit of butter or vegetable oil in a frying pan over medium heat. Use a soup or dessert spoon to ladle the batter into the hot pan. Cook for 2 or 3 minutes, until small bubbles appear around the edges. Flip the pancakes and cook for another 2 minutes. Place them on a plate and keep them warm in the oven while you make the rest.

Serve with maple syrup or this amazing blueberry syrup.

See overleaf for Blueberry Syrup

Blueberry Syrup

2 cups (500 ml) blueberries, fresh
    or frozen, thawed and drained
½ cup (125 ml) + ¼ cup (60 ml) water
½ cup (125 ml) maple syrup
2 Tbsp (30 ml) fresh lemon juice
½ tsp (2 ml) lemon zest
½ tsp (2 ml) vanilla extract
2 Tbsp (30 ml) cornstarch

In a small saucepan, toss the berries, the ½ cup (125 ml) of water, maple syrup, lemon juice and zest and vanilla, stir and bring to a boil. Reduce the heat so the mixture just simmers. Stirring occasionally, allow it to cook until some of the blueberries begin to burst.

In a small bowl, place the cornstarch and the ¼ cup (60 ml) of water and mix to form a thick paste. Stir this paste into your blueberry mixture and blend well. Keep simmering for another 2 or 3 minutes, stirring occasionally, until you have the desired thickness.

Remove from the heat and pour into whatever little serving vessel you're bringing to the table. This keeps for 1 week in an airtight container in the refrigerator.

WHAT'S SO GREAT ABOUT BERRIES? A superfood you don't need to sneak into your kid's diet? That's what I'm talking about! Berries are juicy rock stars, and the most common—blueberries, strawberries and raspberries—all come loaded with antioxidant vitamins C and K (which also benefits your bones) and fiber. Berries support cardio-vascular health by reducing cholesterol and, in some cases, helping our bodies absorb less fat. Given the natural sweetness of berries, you may be surprised by their low glycemic index (the measure of how blood sugars are increased by a food) and by their ability to slow the absorption of glucose found in other foods. Freezing berries does not diminish their nutritional impact so even in the depths of winter you can add them to smoothies and muffins or throw a handful on top of a bowl of cereal or porridge. CM

Breakfast Math

WE'RE NOT EVEN GOING TO SAY IT. You *know* what they say about breakfast. Well, here's the truth behind the cliché. For your kids to spend their mornings alert and happy (and for you to not require three coffees to make it to 11 a.m.) you need a breakfast that delivers on two counts: blood sugar and brain function. Luckily, both can be addressed by the same nutritional duo: complex carbohydrates and proteins. The carb-centric breakfasts that you make when you're in a hurry—toast, cereal—just don't cut it. Adding protein to the mix provides the one-two punch you're after. Because the body burns proteins more slowly than it does carbs, proteins keep you feeling full longer. Proteins also deliver stimulating tyrosine to the brain, whereas complex carbohydrates calm the brain with tryptophan. In combination they create brain function that is both calm and alert. We hope you had a good breakfast before reading this. CM

Egg Bakes

FEEDING KIDS IS SO MUCH ABOUT MARKETING. It's all in the sell. Clearly, this dish is just eggs and toast. But how much more fun (and not much more effort) is it if the eggs are in their own little toast cups? Feel free to jazz these up with sliced mushrooms, a bit of spinach or some grated cheese. And if you've got people coming over and want to simplify your morning, you can make the toast cups the night before and just put them in an airtight container overnight. CM

Prep time: 5 minutes
Total time: 35 minutes
Makes: 4 servings

4 slices whole grain bread
2 Tbsp (30 ml) butter, softened
4 eggs
Salt and pepper

Preheat the oven to 375°F (190°C).

Trim the crusts off your bread. Use a rolling pin to flatten the slices as much as you can. Butter both sides of each piece of bread, then gently press each slice into the cup of a muffin tin. Place the muffin tin on a baking sheet to make it easier to get it in and out of the oven, and put some water in the empty cups to avoid burning.

Pop the tin into the oven for 10 minutes, until the bread is just beginning to turn golden (but not too brown since you're going to bake them again!). Remove from the oven.

Crack an egg into each little nest. Top with a little salt and pepper. Place the tray back in the oven for about 20 minutes. Keep an eye on them at the end. There's nothing worse than a dried-out egg yolk. (At least to me.)

Remove from the oven. Use a butter knife to gently remove the egg bakes from the muffin tin. Serve with a side of greens or fruit salad.

Tortilla Scramble

When my husband, Ben, is on weekend breakfast duty, we give pancakes a rest in favor of this super-satisfying eggy meal. If you're feeling fancy you can serve this with a sprig of cilantro and a side of sour cream. What you can't do is make it pretty because it just isn't. But who cares when something tastes this good? CM

Prep time: 10 minutes

Total time: 25 minutes

Makes: 4 servings

8 small corn tortillas

4 pieces bacon

2 Tbsp (30 ml) olive oil

4 eggs

½ cup (125 ml) shredded cheddar cheese

1–2 Tbsp (15–30 ml) salsa

8–9 cherry tomatoes, diced

½ avocado, diced

Cut each of your tortillas into 8. The pieces will look like corn chips. Chop the bacon into small pieces. Warm the olive oil in a frying pan over medium heat, then add the tortilla chips and bacon. Allow them to sizzle and crisp up, giving it all a stir every few minutes.

In a large bowl, whisk the eggs, then stir in the shredded cheese and salsa.

Pour the egg mixture over the crispy bacon and chips. Stir everything around in there—you're after a scramble, not a frittata. Just as the eggs begin to set, add the tomatoes and avocado and stir. And you're done.

Baked French Toast
with Crumble Topping

I f OUR SWEET POTATO FRENCH TOAST is for weekdays, then this baby is all about the weekend. It's also a great dish for entertaining. It requires time to rest in the refrigerator, so you have no choice but to put it together the night before you serve it. In other words, you're laughing on the day your guests arrive. Plus, the outrageous crumble topping is a real crowd-pleaser. LK

Prep time: 10 minutes

Total time: 50 minutes

(plus overnight refrigeration)

Makes: 4 servings

French Toast

1 loaf challah, sliced

8 eggs

2 cups (500 ml) milk

⅓ cup (80 ml) brown sugar

2 tsp (10 ml) vanilla extract

1 tsp (5 ml) ground cinnamon

1 tsp (5 ml) butter, for greasing the dish

Crumble Topping

1 cup (250 ml) rolled multigrain oats

½ cup (125 ml) chopped pecans

½ cup (125 ml) chopped almonds

¼ cup (60 ml) brown sugar

½ cup (125 ml) cold butter

Warm maple syrup or agave nectar, for serving

Slice your challah into 1-inch (2.5 cm) thick pieces. Discard the end slices and then arrange the bread in two slightly overlapping rows in a greased 9- x 13-inch (3.5 L) casserole dish.

In a large mixing bowl, whisk the eggs, milk, sugar, vanilla and cinnamon. Pour this mixture over the bread, being sure to cover each piece completely. Cover with plastic wrap and refrigerate overnight.

Preheat the oven to 350°F (180°C).

Remove the dish from the refrigerator and allow it to sit for a few minutes. Meanwhile, in a medium-size bowl, mix together the oats, pecans, almonds and sugar. Grate the cold butter into this mixture. Using your hands, work the butter into the mix, creating bean-size crumbs. Remove the plastic wrap from the casserole dish and sprinkle crumble overtop the eggy bread.

Place the dish in the center of the oven to bake for 35 to 40 minutes, until the bread is lightly browned and the eggy mixture is bubbling.

Serve with warm maple syrup or agave nectar.

Biscuits Two Ways

FEW THINGS WARM UP your home like the smell of biscuits baking in the oven first thing in the morning. Whether you're having friends over for brunch or just laying out an easy, help-yourself spread, this combo of sweet and savory pastries is always a winner. But you don't have to wait for the weekend to enjoy this deliciousness. Cut the dough into rounds, place on a parchment-covered baking sheet and pop the sheet in the freezer until the rounds are firm (about an hour or so), then get them into a ziplock bag. Add an extra 5 minutes to their baking time and you'll be a hero on an otherwise gloomy Wednesday morning. CM

See overleaf for recipes

Strawberry Biscuits

Prep time: 25 minutes

Total time: 40 minutes

Makes: 6 biscuits each way

½ cup (125 ml) cold unsalted butter

2 ½ cups (625 ml) spelt flour

1 Tbsp (15 ml) baking powder

1 Tbsp (15 ml) sugar

½ tsp (2 ml) salt

1 cup (250 ml) strawberries, washed,
     hulled and chopped

2 eggs

¾ cup (185 ml) + 1 Tbsp (15 ml) milk

Get your butter into the freezer. You want it in there for 15 or 20 minutes before you plan to use it. Trust me. Preheat the oven to 400°F (200°C). Line a baking sheet with parchment paper. Whisk together the flour, baking powder, sugar and salt in a large bowl.

Take the butter out of the freezer and grate it with a cheese grater. It creates perfect, small bits of butter. (Thanks for my all-time favorite baking tip, Martha Stewart!) Add your butter ribbons to the flour mixture. You can use a fork or your fingers to gently toss the butter around with the flour until each piece gets coated and you create a course meal. Now add your chopped strawberries. Toss the mixture again to spread the berries throughout.

Whisk 1 egg and ¾ cup (185 ml) of the milk together in a small bowl. Add to the flour and butter mixture and mix to combine. It will be a wet dough. Don't overmix!

Dust a clean surface very well with spelt flour. Turn your dough onto the surface (you may want to sprinkle a bit more spelt flour on top). Pat the dough down with your hand until it's about 1 inch (2.5 cm) thick. Using a small juice glass that's been dipped in flour, cut out circles of dough and place them on the prepared baking sheet.

Mix the remaining egg with 1 Tbsp (15 ml) of milk and brush overtop the biscuits. You could sprinkle a pinch of sugar on each if you want an extra bit of sweetness. Pop into the oven for 15 minutes.

Bacon and Chive Biscuits

Prep time: 25 minutes
Total time: 40 minutes
Makes:　6 biscuits each way

½ cup (125 ml) cold butter
2 ½ cups (625 ml) spelt flour
1 Tbsp (15 ml) baking powder
½ tsp (2 ml) salt
½ cup (125 ml) grated Parmesan cheese
½ cup (125 ml) crumbled crisp bacon
　　(about 3 strips)
¼ cup (60 ml) chopped chives
¾ cup (185 ml) buttermilk
　　(or 1 Tbsp/15 ml white vinegar added to
　　¾ cup/185 ml milk and left to stand
　　for 10 minutes)
2 eggs
1 Tbsp (15 ml) milk

Place the butter in the freezer 15 to 20 minutes before you plan to use it. Preheat the oven to 400°F (200°C). Line a baking sheet with parchment paper. In a large bowl, whisk together the flour, baking powder and salt.

Grate the very cold butter with a cheese grater. Put the ribbons of butter into the flour mixture and gently toss it with a fork or your fingers until each piece of butter is coated and you have a coarse meal. Now toss in the cheese, bacon and chives.

In a small bowl, mix the buttermilk with 1 egg. Pour the egg and milk mixture into the flour. Mix to combine well but do not overmix.

Sprinkle a generous amount of spelt flour onto your work surface and pat out the dough until it's 1 inch (2.5 cm) thick. Using a small juice glass that's been dipped in flour, cut out the biscuits and place them on the prepared baking sheet.

Whisk the remaining egg with 1 Tbsp (15 ml) of milk and brush overtop the biscuits. Pop them in the oven for 15 minutes.

Brunch Party

BRUNCH IS THE NEW DINNER PARTY—
at least when it comes to socializing with
friends who also have kids. Everyone is fresh,
there are no bedtimes to worry about and the
food is so universally popular the kids may
even stay at the table for a minute or two.
Many brunch dishes can be made in advance,
making the meal much less stressful and
allowing you time to relax and enjoy your
guests. Sounds like a party to us. **LK & CM**

MENU

Pomegranate Rosemary Cocktail

Simple Prosciutto Strata

Fennel Citrus Salad

Sweet Potato Hash Browns

Plum and Peach German Pancake

Pomegranate Rosemary Cocktail

THIS CHEERY COCKTAIL came to us from my sister-in-law, Amanda Digges, who is both a chef and a fan of entertaining. Kids will love this pomegranate fizz made with sparkling cider, while their parents may enjoy a white wine or champagne variation. **LK**

Prep time: 10 minutes
Total time: 15 minutes
Makes: 10–12 drinks

2 cups (500 ml) water
1 cup (250 ml) agave nectar
    (or 2 cups/500 ml white sugar)
4 sprigs fresh rosemary
1 ½ cups (375 ml) unsweetened
    pomegranate juice
750 ml bottle sparkling white wine
    or champagne
    or 750 ml bottle sparkling cider
1 pomegranate, peeled
    and seeds separated out

Place the water, agave nectar or sugar and rosemary in a small saucepan and bring to a boil. Simmer, uncovered, for 5 minutes. Remove from the heat, let steep until cooled, then strain through a fine-mesh sieve. This simple syrup will keep in an airtight container in the refrigerator for 1 to 2 weeks.

Combine the pomegranate juice with ¼ cup (60 ml) of the simple syrup (adjust to your taste). Fill a champagne flute about one-third of the way up with simple syrup mixture and top it off with sparkling white wine. Garnish with a few pomegranate seeds.

Simple Prosciutto Strata

T HIS STRATA IS PERFECT for entertaining since all the work is done the night before. In the morning you just get it in the oven and forget about it until it starts to fill your home with its amazing aroma. CM

Prep time: 20 minutes
Total time: 1 hour 5 minutes
             (plus overnight refrigeration)
Makes: 12 servings

1 Tbsp (15 ml) olive oil
1 onion, chopped
2 cloves garlic, minced
1 bunch baby spinach,
    washed and trimmed
1 loaf rustic French or Italian bread,
    cubed (you might not use
    the whole loaf)
6–8 slices prosciutto
1 cup (250 ml) grated fontina cheese
1 cup (250 ml) grated Parmesan cheese
8 eggs
2 ½ cups (625 ml) milk
2 Tbsp (30 ml) Dijon mustard
Pepper

In a medium-sized frying pan, heat the olive oil over medium heat. Add the onion and garlic and let soften for about 3 minutes. Toss in the spinach and move it around so it gets coated with the oil. Allow the spinach to wilt. Take the pan off the heat and set aside.

Get out a 9- x 13-inch (3.5 L) baking dish and spread half the bread cubes along the bottom in a single layer. Now place half the spinach mixture over the bread. Place three or four slices of prosciutto on top of the spinach mixture. Sprinkle half of each cheese over everything. Repeat.

In a large bowl, whisk together the eggs, milk, Dijon and a couple of grinds of pepper. Gently pour the egg mixture over the bread. Don't worry if it doesn't all get moistened, the bread will drink up the egg mixture as it sits. Cover the whole thing in plastic wrap and place in the refrigerator overnight.

In the morning, preheat the oven to 375°F (190°C).

Pull the strata out of the refrigerator and place it on the counter while the oven heats up. Bake for 45 to 55 minutes, until the top is golden brown. Allow the strata to cool just a bit before cutting it into squares. It's excellent later as a cold snack, too.

Fennel Citrus Salad

THIS SALAD with its bracing dressing is a light addition to a table of warm and hearty dishes. CM

Prep time: 20 minutes
Total time: 20 minutes
Makes: 6 servings

Salad
1 fennel bulb
2 naval oranges
2 grapefruits
1 bunch watercress
2 cups (500 ml) pomegranate seeds

Dressing
¼ cup (60 ml) fresh orange juice
¼ cup (60 ml) fresh grapefruit juice
1 Tbsp (15 ml) fresh lemon juice
1 tsp (5 ml) lemon zest
⅓ cup (80 ml) olive oil
1 Tbsp (15 ml) finely chopped cilantro
Salt and pepper

Peel off the tough outer layer of the fennel and slice off the root end. Use a mandoline to thinly slice the fennel (or just do your best to make the thinnest possible slices with a sharp knife) and then set it aside.

You could simply peel and segment the oranges and grapefruit and that would be fine. But what's much nicer to eat is citrus that has been supremed (membrane removed). It's messy but easy. Slice a small piece off the top and bottom of the fruit and lay it down on one of its flat ends on a cutting board. Use a very sharp chef's knife to cut away the rind and as much pith (that white stuff that clings to the fruit) as you can. Now, using a bowl to catch the juices, hold the fruit in one hand and use the other to hold your knife and carefully slice inside each segment line. As you cut down either side of each segment it will slide away from the fruit. Work your way around the fruit until it gets too tricky to hold.

Wash and roughly chop the watercress.

Make the dressing by placing the fruit juices, lemon zest, oil, cilantro and salt and pepper to taste in a jar and giving them a good shake.

Place the salad ingredients on a platter and gently toss with half the dressing. Serve with the extra dressing on the side.

Sweet Potato Hash Browns

LOVE THE SWEET AND SAVORY blend of flavors in this healthy version of the breakfast classic. CM

Prep time: 30 minutes
Total time: 50 minutes
Makes: about 2 cups (500 ml)

3 cups (750 ml) sweet potato dice
    (1 large peeled sweet potato
    should do it)
¼ cup (60 ml) maple syrup
1 Tbsp (15 ml) minced fresh rosemary
Salt and pepper
3 Tbsp (45 ml) olive oil
1 medium onion, diced small

Bring a large pot of water to the boil. Blanch the sweet potato cubes for 2 minutes. Drain and rinse them under cold water. Drain well. Place the potatoes in a bowl. Add the maple syrup, rosemary and salt and pepper to taste and give everything a good toss. Put the bowl in the refrigerator for at least 15 minutes.

In a large frying pan, warm up the olive oil and add the onion. Just as it begins to soften, add the sweet potatoes and any liquid that's collected at the bottom of the bowl. Sauté over medium-high heat for 15 to 20 minutes, stirring occasionally. Be gentle or you'll end up with mashed sweet potatoes (which would taste just as good but isn't what you're after). You want everything to get really brown and I'm sorry, but the bottom of your pan will get brown, too. Taste to see if you need a bit more salt and pepper. Serve family-style from a nice big bowl.

Plum and Peach German Pancake

THIS IS AN ENTERTAINER'S DREAM. Like other German pancake recipes, our version is made with pantry essentials, takes nearly no time to prepare and still looks impressive. Unlike traditional recipes, this one leaves off the powdered sugar and berry topping and offers plums and peaches instead. But feel free to dress this light dish with any in-season fruit. (And serve it straight from the pan, not the way we did for our fancy photo.) LK

Prep time: 20 minutes
Total time: 40 minutes
Makes: 4 servings

2 Tbsp (30 ml) unsalted butter
6 eggs
1 cup (250 ml) milk
½ tsp (2 ml) almond extract
¼ tsp (1 ml) sugar
¼ tsp (1 ml) salt
1 cup (250 ml) spelt flour
1 peach, pitted and thinly sliced
1 plum, pitted and thinly sliced

Preheat the oven to 425°F (220°C).

Put the butter in a 12-inch (30 cm) round ovenproof frying pan or skillet and place in the oven until butter melts, about 2 minutes.

In a food processor, place the eggs, milk, almond extract, sugar and salt, and mix until blended. Add the flour and mix again.

Remove the pan from the oven and swirl the butter around to coat the entire inside surface (yep, up the sides and all over the bottom). Pour the batter into the dish. Using a light touch, arrange the peach and plum slices, alternating in a circular pattern, overtop the batter. Place the pan in the oven and bake until the pancake is puffed and the fruit is tender, about 20 minutes. Remove from the oven, allow the pancake to rest for a few minutes and then serve.

LUNCH IN

Deconstructed French Onion Soup

Roasted Tomato and Garlic Soup with Grilled Cheese Croutons

Egg Drop Soup

Corn Pancakes

Classic Chicken or Fish Fingers

Cornmeal-Crusted Fish Sammie

Veggie Sloppy Joes

Grilled Cheese Three Ways

Nizzarda Salad

Sweet Potato Mac & Cheese

Old-Fashioned Mac & Cheese with Kale Breadcrumbs

Mini Kale and Parmesan Quiche with Phyllo Pastry Crust

Mini Kale Pizzas

Phyllo Tofu Parcels

LUNCH OUT

Mini Ham and Pepper Quiche

Salad on a Stick

Turkey, White Bean and Barley Chili

Rock Star Pasta e Fagioli

Risotto, Spinach and Kale Cakes with Parmesan

Sandwich Sushi

Sandwich Safari

Avocado, Lettuce and Tomato Sandwich (aka the ALT)

Deconstructed French Onion Soup

Growing up, we'd know we were having a fancy dinner if my mom pulled out the handled French onion soup bowls. It's got to be one of the most satisfying meals I know, but it's not always the easiest thing for small kids to manage. So I decided to make that big piece of melted cheese and bread into more kid-friendly croutons. I don't know if my kids think of this dish as fancy, but we all love it on a winter weekend. CM

Prep time: 10 minutes

Total time: 40 minutes

Makes: 4 servings

2 onions

2 Tbsp (30 ml) butter

1 clove garlic, minced

2 tsp (10 ml) sugar

1 Tbsp (15 ml) fresh thyme,
      leaves picked off the stems

Salt and pepper

1 Tbsp (15 ml) all-purpose flour

1 Tbsp (15 ml) balsamic vinegar

4 cups (1 L) low-sodium chicken stock

½ baguette

½ cup (125 ml) shredded gruyère

½ cup (125 ml) grated Parmesan cheese

Trim the ends off the onions and peel off the skins. Cut each onion in half lengthwise. Lie each half flat on a cutting board and then cut the thinnest slices you can (mind your fingers!). Depending on the size of the onions, you might even want to cut the slices in half.

In a large saucepan or Dutch oven, melt the butter over medium heat. Add the onions, garlic, sugar, thyme and salt and pepper to taste. Give it all a good stir and let it sweat for 15 to 20 minutes, stirring every few minutes. The onions will become very soft and caramelized but don't let them get too dark.

Sprinkle the flour over the onions and stir to make sure they all get coated. Now add the vinegar and 1 cup (250 ml) of the stock. Stir well, scraping the bottom of the pot to lift up any delicious bits stuck there. Add the rest of the stock. Simmer uncovered for 10 minutes.

Set the oven to broil. Cut your baguette into 1 inch (2.5 cm) slices. Lay the bread on a baking sheet. Mix the two cheeses together and sprinkle a layer of cheese over each piece of bread. Pop the baking sheet under the broiler on the top rack and keep an eye on it. You want the cheese to bubble and the bread to turn golden but it will happen fast. Pull the bread out and allow to cool a bit before cutting each piece of bread into 1 inch- (2.5 cm) squared chunks. Ladle the soup into bowls, top with the cheesey croutons and serve.

Roasted Tomato and Garlic Soup
with Grilled Cheese Croutons

WHEN I WAS LITTLE, my dad's answer to everything that ailed me was garlic. Laura's getting a cold? Give her garlic. Laura's got a toothache? Get out the garlic. Well, Dad, you were right. My version of the classic winter combo—grilled cheese and tomato soup—features a bowl of tomato goodness loaded with my dad's trusted garlic, and is perfect for children who have to fend off whatever heinous illness is ripping through the school. P.S. I also don't run with scissors. LK

Prep time: 1 hour
Total time: 1 hour 30 minutes
Makes: 4 servings

8 plum tomatoes, halved
6 cloves garlic, peeled
3 Tbsp (45 ml) extra virgin olive oil
Salt and pepper
3 Tbsp (45 ml) unsalted butter, divided
½ cup (125 ml) chopped sweet onion
2 Tbsp (30 ml) chopped fresh rosemary
4 cups (1L) low-sodium vegetable broth
1 Tbsp (15 ml) spelt flour

Grilled Cheese Croutons
2 slices spelt or multigrain bread
1 tsp (5 ml) unsalted butter
¼ cup (60 ml) shredded cheddar cheese

Preheat the oven to 400°F (200°C).

In a medium bowl, toss the tomatoes and whole cloves of garlic with olive oil as well as salt and pepper to taste. Transfer into a large baking dish. Roast the tomatoes for 1 hour, stirring occasionally.

Remove the dish from the oven and let cool for a few minutes.

Melt 2 Tbsp (30 ml) of the butter in a large saucepan over medium heat. Add the onion and rosemary and sauté until the onion is translucent. Add the broth and the roasted tomatoes and garlic. Simmer uncovered for about 20 minutes, stirring occasionally.

Working in batches, transfer the soup to a blender and purée. Return the soup to the saucepan set over low heat. In a small frying pan, melt the remaining 1 Tbsp (15 ml) of butter over low heat. Add the flour and whisk continuously until blended to make a roux. Add the roux to the soup, mix to combine well and season to taste with salt and pepper. Allow to simmer uncovered for 3 more minutes.

Meanwhile, heat a greased frying pan over medium heat. Butter the bread. Place one slice, butter side down, in the pan and arrange the cheese on top. Top with the other slice, butter side up. Cook the sandwich until the cheese melts and the bread is golden brown on both sides. Remove from the pan and slice into small, bite-size pieces, triangles or cubes, whatever shape wins in your family. Ladle the soup into bowls. Dress with grilled cheese bits and serve.

Egg Drop Soup

DON'T REMEMBER A LOT about my father's mother, but I do remember she had a wicked sense of humor and went out of her way to make me laugh. An Italian immigrant to North America, my grandmother was also a wonderful cook. This is an easy but satisfying soup she used to make for her family. Scarlett and I have spent many a chilly afternoon sharing a bowl and a lot of good laughs. LK

Prep time: 10 minutes

Total time: 20 minutes

Makes: 4 servings

2 Tbsp (30 ml) unsalted butter

½ cup (125 ml) trimmed and chopped
     asparagus

¼ cup (60 ml) chopped onion

4 cups (1 L) low-sodium chicken broth

2 eggs

¼ cup (60 ml) grated Parmesan cheese,
     plus extra for garnish

Sea salt and pepper

In a large pot, melt the butter, then add asparagus and onion. Sauté until the vegetables begin to soften but are still crisp. Add the broth and bring to a simmer. Allow to simmer uncovered for 5 to 7 minutes.

Meanwhile, in a small bowl, beat the eggs and add the cheese. Reduce the heat under the pot and then drizzle the egg mixture into the broth. Gently stir until the eggs are cooked and look like ribbons, less than 1 minute. Add salt and pepper to taste.

Ladle into bowls, sprinkle with Parmesan and serve.

Corn Pancakes

'M PRETTY STRICT about my "only once a week" and "only on the weekend" rules for pancakes. If I wasn't, my kids would clamor for pancakes every morning. But once in a while I like to blow their minds by announcing that for lunch we're having . . . breakfast (this is effective at dinner, too). I love these savory cornmeal pancakes—they're really satisfying without being heavy and they have a great texture. CM

Prep time: 25 minutes
Total time: 45 minutes
Makes: 4 servings

1 cup (250 ml) frozen corn
2 eggs
2 cups (500 ml) buttermilk
    (or 2 Tbsp/30 ml white vinegar
    + 2 cups/500 ml milk, left to
    stand for 10 minutes)
2 Tbsp (30 ml) vegetable oil,
    plus a bit for the pan
1 ½ cups (375 ml) cornmeal
½ cup (125 ml) all-purpose flour
1 tsp (5 ml) baking soda
1 tsp (5 ml) baking powder
1 tsp (5 ml) salt
1 tsp (5 ml) sugar
4 scallions, trimmed and chopped
    from white to beginning of green

Pour the frozen corn into a small bowl and set aside to thaw. Separate the eggs and whip the whites into soft peaks.

In another bowl, mix the egg yolks with the buttermilk and oil.

In yet another bowl (sorry about all the bowls!), mix together the cornmeal, flour, baking soda, baking powder, salt and sugar.

Add the egg yolk mixture to the dry ingredients and stir to combine. Stir in the thawed corn and scallions. Gently fold in the egg whites. Allow the batter to stand for 10 minutes before cooking.

Heat a small amount of vegetable oil in a large frying pan over medium heat. Pour ¼ cup (60 ml) of batter for each pancake into the hot pan, allow bubbles to form along the edges of the pancakes, flip and cook for a couple of minutes. Serve with tzatziki and salsa.

Classic Chicken or Fish Fingers

THERE ARE FORCES that would have you believe children will only consume food that's been cut up small, breaded and then fried beyond recognition. But that doesn't stop Laura and me from trying to rescue fingers—fish and chicken—from such a sad fate. Over time we've tweaked our coatings to make them a bit more interesting, and of course you could use different seasonings. We like the extra crunch you get from using panko, Japanese-style breadcrumbs, but the recipe will work just as well with regular breadcrumbs. CM

Prep time for both: 15 minutes
Total time for chicken: 30 minutes
Total time for fish: 25 minutes
Makes: 4 servings
                  per option

Chicken Fingers
2 boneless, skinless chicken breasts
1 egg
½ cup (125 ml) panko breadcrumbs
    or traditional dried breadcrumbs
½ cup (125 ml) grated Parmesan cheese
1 tsp (15 ml) lemon zest
Salt and pepper

Fish Fingers
2 tilapia fillets
1 egg
½ cup (125 ml) panko breadcrumbs
    or traditional dried breadcrumbs
½ cup (125 ml) shredded
    unsweetened coconut
Salt and pepper

Preheat the oven to 400°F (200°C).

Cut the chicken or fish in half lengthwise and then horizontally into strips about 1 ½ inches (4 cm) wide.

Whisk the egg in a wide, shallow bowl. On a plate, gently mix together the breadcrumbs with the seasonings.

Dip the fingers of chicken or fish into the egg and then dredge them in the breadcrumb mixture. Place the coated fingers on a clean plate.

Brush the tiniest bit of olive oil on a nonstick baking sheet and line up the fingers. Bake the fish for 10 minutes and the chicken for 15 minutes, flipping once, about halfway through cooking time. Serve with steamed veggies.

Cornmeal-Crusted Fish Sammie

'D EAT THIS SANDWICH any time but it's particularly great on a summer weekend. It's quick and easy to make but if you whipped up a crunchy side of coleslaw it would be special enough to serve to guests. It's all about the mayo, which gets a little zing from Sriracha, a not-too-spicy sweet chili sauce from Thailand (it's not health food but it's no worse for you than ketchup and a little goes a long way). Don't worry, if you go out and buy a bottle you'll be using it all the time—it's addictive stuff! CM

Prep time: 10 minutes
Total time: 20 minutes
Makes: 4 sandwiches

¼ cup (60 ml) cornmeal
¼ cup (60 ml) finely chopped
   fresh parsley
¼ tsp (1 ml) chili powder
¼ (1 ml) salt
¼ (1 ml) pepper
2 tilapia fillets
2 Tbsp (30 ml) vegetable oil
1 cup (250 ml) mayonnaise
1 ½ Tbsp (22 ml) ketchup
1 Tbsp (15 ml) Sriracha
4 whole grain buns
4 romaine leaves, chopped
2 tomatoes, sliced

Place the cornmeal, parsley, chili powder and salt and pepper on a plate, stir to combine and spread the mixture out evenly.

Rinse the fish and pat the fillets dry. Press each side into the cornmeal mixture to coat well.

Heat the vegetable oil in a large frying pan over medium heat. Place the fish in the oil and cook for about 5 minutes on one side, carefully flip and cook for about 3 minutes on the other side. (The fish should be opaque and the cornmeal should have formed a nice crust.)

While the fish is cooking, mix together the mayo, ketchup and Sriracha in a small bowl. You can add a bit more Sriracha if you've got older or more adventurous kids.

Remove the fish from the pan and place it on a cutting board. Break it up into large pieces. Slice open the buns and spread a generous amount of mayo on each side. Stack up the lettuce, tomato and fish. You'll probably have a bit of mayo left over but you'll be glad you do—it's delicious on any sandwich. It will keep covered in the fridge for 1 week.

Veggie Sloppy Joes

THIS SLOPPY JOE is my childhood on a plate. Growing up in the '70s, you just couldn't escape this meaty dish. Since it's such a comfort food, Ceri and I decided to go retro and bring back the sloppy. We've updated it, of course, for a more health-conscious family, substituting all that ground beef with a flavor-rich black bean sauce. **LK**

Prep time: 10 minutes
Total time: 35 minutes
Makes: 6 servings

1 Tbsp (15 ml) olive oil
1 medium onion, diced
½ cup (125 ml) diced carrots
1 cup (250 ml) trimmed and
      diced mushrooms
¼ tsp (1 ml) ground cumin
¼ tsp (1 ml) paprika
3 cups (750 ml) canned black beans,
      drained and rinsed
1 cup (250 ml) prepared tomato sauce
2 Tbsp (30 ml) red wine vinegar
1 tsp (5 ml) Dijon mustard
1 tsp (5 ml) maple syrup
Salt and pepper
6 whole wheat hamburger buns
½ cup (125 ml) shredded cheddar
      or Monterey Jack cheese

Heat the olive oil in a large frying pan over medium heat. Add the onion and carrots and sauté until they begin to soften, about 5 minutes. Now add the mushrooms, cumin and paprika. Stir everything together and allow the mushrooms to soften, 2 to 3 minutes.

Add the beans, tomato sauce, vinegar, mustard and syrup, and allow to simmer and thicken for about 15 minutes. Taste and add salt and pepper if you like.

Toast the hamburger buns (to make those Joes a bit less sloppy). Spoon a generous amount of the bean mixture onto the bottom half of each bun and sprinkle with a good pinch of shredded cheese. Put that hamburger lid on top and serve.

Grilled Fontina with Grapes

Grilled Cheese Three Ways

THERE ARE REALLY FEW THINGS that beat coming home from a weekend morning of groceries, soccer practice and ballet class than knowing that a plate of gooey, cheesey goodness is moments away. Of course, there's nothing wrong with a traditional grilled cheese, but you already know how to make that. Here are a few delicious variations Laura and I keep in heavy rotation. CM

See overleaf for recipes ●━━━●

Grilled Cream Cheese with Jam

Prep time: 10 minutes
Total time: 20 minutes
Makes: 2 servings

1 Tbsp (15 ml) butter
¼ cup (60 ml) cream cheese
2 Tbsp (30 ml) raspberry jam
4 slices multigrain bread

In a large frying pan, melt the butter over medium heat.

Spread half the cream cheese and then half the jam on a slice of bread. Repeat with a second slice. Place the bread, cheese side up, in the pan. Top with the remaining bread.

Allow the underside of the bread to become golden, 5 minutes, flip and repeat on the other side. Remove from the pan, cut as required and serve.

Grilled Cheese with Garlic Apples

Prep time: 10 minutes
Total time: 20 minutes
Makes: 2 servings

1 Tbsp (15 ml) butter
1 clove garlic, minced
1 Gala apple, peeled and thinly sliced
4 slices multigrain bread
½ cup (125 ml) crumbled aged cheddar
   cheese

In a large frying pan, melt the butter over medium heat. Add the garlic and sauté for 2 minutes, until it becomes translucent. Add the apple slices and sauté for 2 minutes to soften. Remove the apple slices and garlic from the pan and set aside.

In the same frying pan, place two slices of bread side by side. Top with cheese and then garlic-apple slices and cap with the other slices of bread.

Cook until the underside of the bread is golden, 5 minutes. Flip. Cook until the cheese is melted and the second side of the bread is golden. Remove from the pan, cut as required and serve.

Grilled Fontina with Grapes

Prep time: 10 minutes

Total time: 20 minutes

Makes: 2 servings

1 Tbsp (15 ml) softened butter

4 slices dark rye bread

2/3 cup (160 ml) shredded fontina cheese

10–12 seedless, red grapes, sliced in
    half lengthwise

2 tsp (10 ml) Dijon mustard

Get all the ingredients ready before you begin because you're going to assemble this beauty right in the pan. Ready?

Butter one side of each slice of bread.

Heat a large frying pan over medium heat and place two slices of bread, butter side down, in the pan. Sprinkle half the cheese over each slice of bread, spreading it out as close as you can get to the edges. Press the grape slices into the cheese. Spread a thin layer of Dijon on the non-buttered side of the other slices of bread. Place those pieces, Dijon-side down, on top of the slices in the pan to make a sandwich. Cook on the first side for 5 minutes.

Use a spatula to lift up each sandwich and apply light pressure with your other hand to keep it together. Quick flip! Allow to cook on the other side for 3 to 5 minutes until the cheese is melty and the bread is crispy.

Remove from the pan and serve in 2 or 4 triangles (depending on your household's feelings about these matters).

WHAT'S SO GREAT ABOUT GARLIC? A root herb, garlic is probably best known for its strong flavor and lasting effects on your breath. However, grab some mints because those little bulbs pack a huge, health-enhancing punch. A member of the allium family (along with leeks and onions), garlic is rich in a compound known as allicin. When the bulb is disturbed through crushing or slicing, allicin is released, and with it not only garlic's powerful taste and aroma but also its enormous benefits for cardiovascular health and the plant's anti-inflammatory and anti-bacterial properties. Since heat diminishes these gains, it's best to let crushed or cut cloves rest for a few minutes before tossing them into the cooking pot. Garlic is also rich in the antioxidant vitamin C, known to fight free radicals in the body. Finally, the phytonutrients in garlic are proven to be effective against infection, and are thought to contribute to lowering the risk of some cancers. LK

Nizzarda Salad

LAURA AND I BOTH LOVE the Nizzarda salad from Terroni, a small chain of amazing Italian restaurants in Toronto. This is our take on the Italian classic. In general, I'm a big fan of meal salads and I hope upon hope that one day my children will be too. For now, they pick around what they like and what they don't like and that's just fine with me. CM

Prep time: 20 minutes
Total time: 25 minutes
Makes: 4 servings

4 eggs
10–12 green beans, trimmed
1 can (14 oz/398 ml) cannellini beans
1 can (5 oz/142 g) tuna
1 small head arugula
4 plum tomatoes
10 olives (I like the wrinkly black
    Moroccan olives but the little niçoise
    ones would be perfect, too)
½ red onion, thinly sliced

Dressing
¼ cup (60 ml) olive oil
2 Tbsp (30 ml) white wine vinegar
1 tsp (5 ml) Dijon mustard
Salt and pepper

Put the eggs in cold water, bring the water to a boil, then remove the pot and let the eggs sit and cook for 12 minutes. Drain and rinse in cold water to stop them from overcooking. Once the eggs are cooled, peel and slice them into quarters.

Blanch the green beans by putting them in a pot of boiling water for about 3 minutes until just tender. Drain and rinse them in cold water so they don't get too soft.

Rinse the cannellini beans and the tuna (particularly if you're using oil-packed tuna, which is not as healthy but so much more delicious than water-packed).

For the dressing, place the olive oil, vinegar, mustard and salt and pepper to taste in a small dish or jar and mix well to combine.

Place the arugula, tomatoes, beans, olives and onion on a platter and toss on some of the dressing. Then arrange chunks of tuna and eggs on top and drizzle a bit more dressing overtop.

Sweet Potato Mac & Cheese

THE WHOLE WHEAT NOODLES and sweet potato up the nutritional score of this recipe, but it's as creamy and satisfying as a more traditional mac and cheese. I first made it when I needed to bring a dish to the Christmas potluck at Esme's daycare a couple of years ago. It's great any time you have to feed a big gang. CM

Prep time: 20 minutes
Total time: 20 minutes
Makes: 8 servings

1 cup (250 ml) sweet potato purée
     (see page 17 or use canned)
3 cups (750 ml) whole wheat macaroni
¼ cup (60 ml) butter
2 Tbsp (30 ml) all-purpose flour
2 cups (500 ml) milk
1 cup (250 ml) shredded cheddar cheese
½ cup (125 ml) grated Parmesan cheese
Salt and pepper
1 cup (250 ml) frozen peas

Cook the pasta according to the package instructions. In a large heavy-bottomed saucepan, melt the butter over medium-low heat. Sprinkle the flour over the butter, stir and allow to cook for a minute or two. Now slowly add the milk, stirring continually to stop the sauce from lumping up. If it's not thickening, nudge the heat up just a bit. Now add the cheeses and stir as they melt. Add the puréed sweet potato and stir well to combine. Taste before seasoning with salt and pepper.

In the last 2 minutes of the pasta's cooking time, add the frozen peas. (Who needs to dirty another pot?) Drain the pasta and peas in a sieve. Pour the cooked pasta and peas into the pot with sauce and give everything a good stir. Serve straight from the pot into bowls.

Old-Fashioned Mac & Cheese
with Kale Breadcrumbs

THIS IS THE HOLY GRAIL of mac and cheese—a rich, creamy middle with a crispy topping all snuggled together warm and bubbly. It actually might be Scarlett's most favorite dish. Are you surprised? I love the flavor the chicken stock lends to it, as well as the vitamin bonus of kale in the topping. It's easy to add vegetables like broccoli, peas and carrots. Just stir them in and enjoy. LK

Prep time: 20 minutes
Total time: 50 minutes
Makes: 8 servings

4 cups (1 L) spelt elbow macaroni
2 large kale leaves
1 tsp (5 ml) grapeseed oil
2 Tbsp (30 ml) unsalted butter
2 Tbsp (30 ml) spelt flour
1 ½ cups (375 ml) milk
¼ cup (60 ml) low-sodium chicken stock
1 cup (250 ml) shredded cheddar cheese
1 ½ cups (375 ml) shredded Monterey
    Jack cheese, divided
1 tsp (5 ml) honey mustard
2 slices dry whole grain bread
½ tsp (2 ml) salt

Preheat the oven to 350°F (180°C).

Cook the pasta according to the package directions. Drain and set aside.

Brush the kale leaves with the oil and place on a baking sheet in the oven for 8 to 10 minutes, or until they're crisp and the edges are brown. Be careful not to burn the leaves.

In a medium-size saucepan, melt the butter over medium-low heat, then slowly add the flour, whisking continuously until it's blended and smooth. Add the milk and chicken stock, and allow to simmer for 5 minutes so the mixture can slowly thicken, stirring occasionally. Add the cheddar, 1 cup (250 ml) of the Monterey Jack cheese and the mustard and remove from the heat. Mix until the cheeses have melted and the mustard has been combined.

Meanwhile, place the bread and kale chips in a blender and whiz until you have the consistency of crumbs you prefer.

Put the cooked pasta in a medium-size casserole dish and mix in the cheese sauce, being sure to coat all the pasta. Sprinkle with the remaining ½ cup (125 ml) of Monterey Jack cheese and then top with the breadcrumbs. Bake in the oven for about 30 minutes, or until the cheese sauce is bubbling and the edges are golden brown.

Switch to Whole Grain Everything

WHENEVER YOU'RE TRYING TO MAKE an improvement to your family's diet, it makes sense to start with what they love. Esme and Julian consume so much pasta, bread and rice that I need them to eat the healthiest versions of those items. A grain—whether we're talking oats, barley, spelt, flax or wheat—is considered whole if left in its entirety. So, the bran, the germ and the endosperm are all there. All that wholeness delivers a health-promoting combination of high fiber, vitamins, minerals and antioxidants. A diet high in whole grains is associated with lower rates of obesity, high cholesterol and diabetes. You do need to make some small adjustments when you switch over to whole grains, though. You need a bit more time to make porridge with rolled oats than with quick-cooking oats. Same for brown rice. I had to try a couple of brands of whole grain pasta before I found one I liked. But my kids? They didn't even notice. CM

Mini Kale and Parmesan Quiche
with Phyllo Pastry Crust

T HIS RECIPE IS AN EMOTIONAL FAVORITE of mine. It was the first dish Scarlett and I created together. She was just three years old, and I was looking for ways to incorporate the nutrient-dense kale into dishes I knew she'd eat. She was already a fan of quiche, so I figured this would be an easy sell. I just needed a way to eliminate the fatty crust and phyllo was the answer. This dish was an instant success with Scarlett as well as with Ceri's children. It also became an SPC site favorite. Ceri and I have many fond memories of making this dish on photo shoots and in television studios while our girls tore apart the joints. However, whenever I think about the history of this simple but wildly nutritious meal, I remember Scarlett's three-year-old face, beaming from her cooking perch, proudly pouring egg mixture into ramekins and all over the counter. **LK**

Prep time: 10 minutes

Total time: 50 minutes

Makes: 4 servings

2 Tbsp (30 ml) olive oil,
  plus extra for brushing
¼ cup (60 ml) chopped onion
3 cloves garlic, chopped
1 ½ lb (680 g) kale
4 sheets phyllo pastry
5 eggs
¾ cup (185 ml) milk
½ cup (125 ml) grated Parmesan cheese
Salt and pepper

For the pesto, in a large frying pan, heat the oil over medium heat. Add the onion and garlic and sauté until translucent, about 3 minutes. Add the kale and coat with the oil mixture. Cover and allow the kale to wilt, until the tough stems are tender, 6 to 8 minutes.

Remove the kale from the pan and place it in a food processor. Process until it has the texture of a fine pesto.

See overleaf for preparation continued

For the quiche, cut the four sheets of phyllo into four equal-size squares. Layer the phyllo squares one by one into four large ramekins, brushing each layer of pastry lightly with oil. (Keep the phyllo sheets between two moist dish towels to prevent them from drying out when you're not actually working with them.)

In a large mixing bowl, beat the eggs. Add the milk then the Parmesan cheese and mix until blended. Add the kale and stir to combine well. Season to taste with salt and pepper.

Pour the egg mixture into the ramekins, leaving about ¼ inch (0.5 cm) at the top. Place the ramekins on a baking sheet and then place on the middle rack of the oven. Bake for 30 to 35 minutes, or until firm. Remove the baking sheet and allow the ramekins to cool before serving to little hands.

WHAT'S SO GREAT ABOUT KALE? Kale is the king of the cruciferous vegetable family, which also includes bok choy, broccoli, cauliflower and Brussels sprouts. A nutritional powerhouse, kale has sky-high levels of antioxidants like vitamins C and A, which help the body to detoxify. Kale also has stellar amounts of vitamin K and flavonoids to combat inflammation. To unleash the leafy vegetable's health benefits, it is recommended that you chop the leaves. LK

Mini Kale Pizzas

ONE LOVELY SPRING DAY, Ceri and I packed a lunch, bought chocolate chip cookies the size of salad plates and headed out for a picnic. The kids picked flowers, crashed neighboring picnics and rolled in the grass. It was a memorable afternoon not only for its ease but also for its food. One of the best things about these simple and enticing pizzas is that you use the leftovers of our kale pesto (page 85) to make them. In fact, I like to double the pesto recipe to ensure I have lots of leftovers to store in my freezer. I store it in 2 Tbsp (30 ml) amounts for easy use in pizzas and pastas. You can thank me later. LK

Prep time: 10 minutes
Total time: 15 minutes
Makes: 4 servings

4 mini pita pockets, halved
Olive oil
2 Tbsp (30 ml) kale pesto (see page 85)
½ cup (125 ml) shredded
    mozzarella cheese
1 Tbsp (15 ml) grated Parmesan cheese

Lay the pita halves on a clean work surface. Drizzle each half with a bit of olive oil. Place 1 tsp (5 ml) of kale pesto on each half and spread, leaving a tiny rim around the edges.

Sprinkle each half with the cheeses.

Toast in a toaster oven until the edges of the pita toast and the cheese melts, about 4 minutes.

Pack the halves into an airtight container with a piece of parchment paper between the layers of pizzas.

Phyllo Tofu Parcels

THIS IS ONE OF MY FAVORITE LUNCHES and it came to me from one of my dearest friends. A fitness trainer and nutritionist buff, Kathy (she also writes the wildly popular *What's So Great About?* column on SPC) has a gluten allergy. As a result, she spends hours in her kitchen free-styling—adjusting recipes so she can enjoy them once again. A strict vegetarian, Kathy created this hybrid spanakopita to include tofu and low-fat cheese—she gets her iron, protein and calcium without the fat. I like to dip them in tzatziki, but I can imagine honey mustard would be great too. LK

Prep time: 25 minutes
Total time: 45 minutes
Makes: about 36 parcels

1 ½ cups (375 ml) fresh baby spinach
1 ½ cups (375 ml) chopped fresh kale
1 large zucchini, roughly chopped
1 large carrot, roughly chopped
1 lb (450 g) brick medium-firm low-fat tofu
1 ½ cups (375 ml) shredded low-fat
    sharp cheddar cheese
1 tsp (5 ml) coriander
3 sheets phyllo pastry
2 tsp (10 ml) coconut oil
    or melted coconut butter
1 Tbsp (15 ml) poppy seeds
    or sesame seeds
1 tsp (5 ml) sea salt

Preheat the oven to 400°F (200°C). Lightly grease a baking sheet with nonstick spray.

Using a food processor with the grater attachment, grate the spinach, kale, zucchini, carrot and tofu. Grate until the vegetables are the size of a pea or smaller.

Transfer the mixture to a bowl and stir in the cheese and coriander. Put the bowl in the refrigerator to chill for 30 minutes.

Take the three sheets of phyllo, lay them out on top of each other and cut them into six squares. Spoon approximately 2 Tbsp (30 ml) of filling onto the middle of each square. Fold the bottom left corner over to the top right, creating a triangle. Fold over the ends to close. Repeat with the remaining squares and filling.

Lay the parcels on the prepared baking sheet. Brush with melted coconut butter or coconut oil, especially at the edges to seal them closed. Sprinkle the parcels with sesame or poppy seeds and sea salt. Place the baking sheet in the oven and bake for about 20 minutes, or until the phyllo is lightly browned and crisp.

Good luck
today!

Mini Ham and Pepper Quiche

WHO SAYS LUNCH has to be a sandwich? Not us. These easy little quiches are a simple way to throw a curve ball into a packed lunch. I make a batch on Sundays and pop them in the freezer. If I place a few, frozen, in Esme's lunch box at night, they're thawed and ready to eat by the time the lunch bell rings the next day. Try other combinations, like tinned salmon and spinach or finely chopped red and yellow bell pepper. CM

Prep time: 10 minutes
Total time: 25 minutes
Makes: 18 mini quiches

⅓ cup (80 ml) cubed ham
⅓ cup (80 ml) sliced green onion
⅓ cup (80 ml) shredded cheddar cheese
2 cherry tomatoes, chopped
3 eggs
½ cup (125 ml) milk
18 premade mini pastry shells

Preheat the oven to 375°F (190°C).

Toss together the ham, onion, cheese and tomatoes in a bowl. Whisk the eggs with the milk in another bowl.

Keeping the pastry shells in their metal wrappers, place them on a baking sheet. Place about 1 Tbsp (15 ml) of the ham and cheese mixture in each of the shells. Gently pour some egg mixture into each, leaving just a bit of space at the top, as the filling will puff up.

Bake for 15 minutes, until the egg is just set. Allow to cool before serving. Once they're completely cool you can stack them in a container for a packed lunch. These will keep in a sealed container in the refrigerator for 3 days and in the freezer for 1 month.

Salad on a Stick

HERE'S ONE OF OUR not-really-a-recipe recipes. Salad on a Stick is more about marketing than it is about some genius combination of ingredients. When you're looking for ways to get kids to eat foods that are feared or loathed, it's always worth thinking about presentation. And remember, everything is just cuter on a stick. Most grocery stores will have two sizes of wooden skewers—go for the smaller of the two. These are perfect for a picnic. CM

Prep time: 20 minutes
Total time: 20 minutes
Makes: 4 sticks each for 1 packed lunch

There's no real trick to this one. Alternate the ingredients on the wooden skewers. Just be sure you put a good firm item on the ends. For instance, the cheese chunks are good as a last item on your Chef on a Stick, as they keep the folded slice of turkey from unfolding.

Caprese on a Stick

12 cherry tomatoes
8 baby bocconcini
12–16 small-ish fresh basil leaves

Chef on a Stick

4 pieces of thinly sliced turkey, cut in half
    and then folded in half
8 cherry tomatoes
8 1-inch (2.5 cm) cubes cheddar cheese
½ avocado, cut into 2-inch (5 cm) chunks with
    a squirt of lemon juice to keep them from browning

Waldorf on a Stick

½ Granny Smith apple, cored and cut into
    2-inch (5 cm) slices
1–2 leaves romaine lettuce, cut into 2-inch (5 cm) strips
1 stick celery, cut into 2-inch (5 cm) slices
8–10 seedless red grapes

Lunches to Keep
Kids Alert

DO YOU EVER HIT A WALL at 3:00 p.m. and wonder how you'll make it through the day without a coffee or something sweet? That was the story of my life until I realized that my mid-afternoon lull was likely caused by my lunch choice. If you have a noontime meal laden with proteins high in the amino acid tryptophan—eggs, meat, milk, bananas—then you're going to sedate your brain. Now imagine that tired and distracted state settling in on your children while they're at school. As parents, we work hard to stack the cards in favor of learning, and that's why fixing a lunch featuring proteins full of the amino acid tyrosine—tuna, seafood, turkey, legumes and tofu are all great sources of tyrosine—is as important as packing their books in their backpacks. Pairing these types of proteins with a balance of complex carbohydrates and a small amount of healthy fats will help ensure your kids want to go back to school rather than back to bed after lunch. LK

Turkey, White Bean and Barley Chili

WE LOVE THIS CHILI for its versatility—it can easily be made vegetarian by subbing in tofu or adding more veggies. Try making a batch on Sunday that you can use for lunches during the week. Or, on a cold night, it's also a satisfying dinner (serve over some thickly sliced grain bread with shaved cheese and a dollop of sour cream) that doubles for lunch the next day. You can adjust the seasoning to suit the various spice barometers in your family. LK

Prep time: 15 minutes
Total time: 45 minutes
Makes: 6 servings

1 Tbsp (15 ml) olive oil
1 onion, finely chopped
3 cloves garlic, minced
1 stick celery, finely chopped
1 green bell pepper, finely chopped
1 lb (450 g) ground turkey
2 Tbsp (30 ml) chili powder
2 tsp (10 ml) ground cumin
½ tsp (2 ml) dried oregano
¼ tsp (1 ml) salt
1 can (8 oz/240 ml) low-sodium
    chicken stock
1 carrot, peeled and chopped
1 cup (250 ml) pearl barley
1 can (14 oz/398 ml) white beans,
    drained and rinsed

Heat the oil in a large Dutch oven over medium heat. Add the onion, garlic, celery and bell pepper. Cook until the onion is translucent and the vegetables are beginning to soften but are still crisp, about 5 minutes.

Add the turkey to the pan, breaking it apart with a wooden spoon. Cook until the turkey is no longer pink, about 6 minutes. Stir in the chili powder, cumin, oregano and salt. Add the chicken stock along with the carrot and barley. Cover and allow to simmer for about 10 minutes, stirring occasionally. Add the beans and mix well. Cover and cook on low heat for 10 to 15 more minutes.

Pour hot water in a thermos so it heats up while you warm up a serving of chili in the morning. Empty out the water, then carefully spoon the hot chili into the thermos. Seal it tight and add it to a lucky lunch box.

Rock Star Pasta e Fagioli

To the traditionalists, I apologize! This is Pasta Fazool by way of a picky preschooler. The name comes from what it did for my ego to create a dinner that made Esme enthusiastically clean her plate. This dish does double duty: dinner one evening becomes the next day's thermos of warm and hearty lunch. CM

Prep time: 20 minutes
Total time: 35 minutes
Makes: 6 servings

3 Tbsp (45 ml) olive oil
1 onion, diced
3 cloves garlic, minced
2–3 stalks celery, chopped
3 medium carrots,
    peeled and thinly sliced
6 mushrooms,
    cleaned and sliced (not too thin)
1 yellow or green zucchini,
    halved and sliced
2 cups (500 ml) low-sodium
    vegetable stock
1 can (14 oz/398 ml) cannellini beans
1 can (28 oz/796 ml) plum tomatoes,
    drained
1 cup (250 ml) whole wheat tubetti pasta
1 tsp (5 ml) dried rosemary
1 tsp (5 ml) dried thyme
Salt and pepper
½ cup (125 ml) grated Parmesan cheese

In a large pot, warm the olive oil over medium heat and then add the onion, garlic and celery. Sauté for about 5 minutes, until the vegetables just become translucent. Add the carrots. Allow them to cook for about 5 minutes before adding the mushrooms and zucchini. Stir and just let the last vegetables begin to soften. Add the stock.

Rinse and drain the cannellini beans and scoop out about ⅓ cup (80 ml). Put these in a bowl and mash them with the back of a fork. It doesn't have to be perfect, the mashed beans are just going to give you a thicker, creamier bowl of soup. Put all the beans in the pot, cover and allow to simmer for about 5 minutes.

Add the drained canned tomatoes to the pot. Break them up a bit with the back of a spoon. Cover and simmer for 5 more minutes.

Now add the pasta, rosemary and thyme. Give everything a good stir before covering again and simmering for 10 minutes. Check the pasta for doneness (you want it to be al dente as it will keep cooking on the way to the table or in the thermos). Add salt and pepper to taste.

Serve with a good pinch of Parmesan. If you're packing this, just sprinkle the cheese on top before putting the lid on the thermos.

Risotto, Spinach and Kale Cakes
with Parmesan

W E THINK THESE LITTLE CAKES have everything going for them, from their portable size to their delicious Parmesan flavor. This hearty risotto also gets a dose of my favorite superfood, kale. Two-bite wonders, they're a great lunch packed up with some fruit and cut vegetables. You can also serve these little bundles alongside eggs at breakfast or as a side with dinner. LK

Prep time: 30 minutes
Total time: 1 hour
Makes: about 8

½ cup (125 ml) arborio rice
1 Tbsp (15 ml) butter
¼ cup (60 ml) chopped onion
3 cloves garlic, minced
1 cup (250 ml) chopped kale,
    fresh or frozen
1 cup (250 ml) chopped spinach,
    fresh or frozen
½ cup (125 ml) grated Parmesan cheese
2 eggs

Preheat the oven to 400°F (200°C). Using a nonstick spray, grease a muffin tin.

Cook the arborio rice according to the package directions. If you're using fresh greens, wash and remove any tough stems then chop. If your greens are frozen, thaw them for a few minutes and squeeze out any liquid.

Meanwhile, in a small frying pan, melt the butter over medium heat. Add the onion and garlic. Sauté for 2 to 3 minutes, or until the onion is translucent. Add the kale and spinach and sauté for about 5 minutes. Transfer this mixture to a food processor and pulse until finely chopped.

Transfer to a medium-size bowl and add the rice and cheese. Beat the eggs and then add to the rice. Stir to combine. Pour the mixture into the prepared muffin tin, leaving about 1 inch (2.5 cm) space at the top. Place in the oven and bake for 18 to 20 minutes, or until the egg is set and the edges are golden brown.

Allow to cool for a few minutes. Loosen the edges with a knife and turn the cakes onto a plate. Store in an airtight container in the refrigerator for up to 4 days.

Sandwich Sushi

SOMETIMES DOING SOMETHING as simple as rolling up an everyday tuna sandwich into sushi can be the difference between a lunch that gets eaten and one that comes home with your kids at the end of the day. I've suggested a few different fillings but really just about anything can become sushi. CM

Prep time: 20 minutes

Total time: 30 minutes

Makes: 1 slice of bread = 3 sushis

A few slices of whole wheat bread

Tuna salad (drained, mixed with
    a bit of mayo and diced pickle)

Egg salad (hard boiled, mashed with
    a bit of mayo and a tiny bit of
    Dijon and diced celery)

Ham

Cheese, shredded

Avocado, cut into small cubes

Almond butter (for a lunch
    not going to school)

Jam

Prepare the fillings the way your family likes them. Just remember to keep all the chopped ingredients (celery, pickle, etc.) on the fine side. You don't want any big chunks to deal with.

Trim the crusts off the bread. Now use a rolling pin to really flatten the bread, particularly at the edges. Spoon about a 1 ½-inch (4 cm) line of filling along one edge of the bread. With the filling side toward you, start rolling away from yourself. Try to keep the roll as tight and snug as possible. Place the first roll, seam side down to pin it closed, on a plate and set aside. Keep rolling. Once you've rolled as many pieces of bread as you want, use a serrated knife to cut the "sushi."

Depending on how large the pieces of bread are, you'll get two or three pieces of sushi per roll. Place them in a container, seam side down, tucking them in close together so they keep from unraveling.

WHAT'S SO GREAT ABOUT AVOCADO? Avocado gets a bad rap as one of the few fruits to be avoided by waist-watching parents. In fact, it's the fats in avocados that make them so healthy. The oleic acid (the kind also found in olives and olive oil) works to improve the body's absorption of phytonutrients—the other nutrients in the fruit and in the foods you eat with it. And while a perfectly ripe avocado is the definition of creaminess, it contains almost half your daily requirement of fiber. CM

Sandwich Safari

A SANDWICH DOESN'T ALWAYS have to mean a piece of meat, a slice of cheese, some greens and a condiment. It can be a combination of snack foods snuggled between bread. In other words, your favorite noshie foods ready for a ride in your lunch box. There are excellent prepared products on the market that can help you put together creative lunches—hummus, baba ghanoush, tabbouleh—so don't feel like you have to make every little thing from scratch. Sandwiches are the perfect vehicle for driving children's imaginations—with no rules on what can and cannot go together, there is no limit to what the little geniuses might come up with. Scarlett loves to dream up recipes. A lot of them aren't ready for printing (unless you like broccoli in your ice cream), but her sandwich ideas have been unquestionably delicious. She's responsible for more than one of the winning combinations suggested below. LK

- Baba ghanoush with cucumber slices and Monterey Jack cheese
- Hummus with sliced Granny Smith apple and feta cheese
- Tuna with diced Granny Smith apples, diced pickle, mayo and a bit of Dijon
- Ricotta cheese mixed with sliced strawberries
- Sliced turkey and farmer's cheese tortilla pinwheels
- Goat cheese with sliced pear and honey
- Cheddar cheese and sliced apple
- Egg salad in mini pita pockets
- Chicken salad with chopped red grapes
- Roasted red bell peppers and goat cheese

- Grilled chicken with avocado and mango
- Tuna, tabbouleh and feta in a pita
- Sliced tomato with bocconcini cheese and basil
- Black bean, avocado and Monterey Jack cheese tortilla wrap
- Avocado, cucumber, shredded carrot and herb cream cheese
- Ham, cheese and apricot preserve
- Ricotta cheese mixed with grated carrot, zucchini and finely chopped red bell pepper
- Mini whole grain waffles filled with cream cheese and strawberry preserve
- Silver dollar whole grain pancakes with apple butter, sliced banana and honey

Hummus with sliced Granny Smith apple and feta cheese

Avocado, Lettuce and Tomato Sandwich
(aka the ALT)

I BELIEVE YOU SHOULDN'T TRY to make a traditionally sinful dish healthy unless you can actually make it taste as good as, if not better than, its wicked beginnings. I think we managed just that with our transformation of the BLT into an ALT. Admittedly, I'm not a bacon fan, but who wouldn't love a mash-up of avocado and torn fresh basil? You can pack this up to go if you put each component of the sammie into its own travel container. **LK**

Prep time: 10 minutes
Total time: 15 minutes
Makes: 2 servings

1 tomato
1 tsp (5 ml) extra virgin olive oil
Sea salt
½ avocado
1 tsp (5 ml) fresh lemon juice
4 basil leaves, torn
4 slices multigrain or spelt bread
6 large leaves Boston bibb lettuce, torn

Slice the tomato, discarding the stem and bottom side, and put the slices on a plate. Coat the tomato with the olive oil and sprinkle with sea salt. Set aside.

Mash the avocado in a medium-size bowl. Add the lemon juice and torn basil. Mix until smooth.

Toast the bread.

To assemble the sandwich, smear about 1 ½ Tbsp (22 ml) of avocado spread on one slice of toasted bread. Add 3 leaves of lettuce and a slice or two of tomato, then top with the second slice of toast. Serve.

Kitchen Sink Granola Bars
Sunflower Oat Balls
Maple Corn Bread
Zucchini Bread
Piña Colada Muffins
Orange Chocolate Mini Muffins

snacks

Whole Grain Blueberry Muffins
Wagamama Cookies
Cocoa Date Bars
Applewich with all the Trimmings
Roasted Pumpkin Seeds
Roasted Chickpeas

Kitchen Sink Granola Bars

I N AN EFFORT TO UP MY SNACK GAME, I concocted this recipe using the leftover ingredients from an ill-fated detox. (That would be the detox I quit after four days, by which stage everyone was becoming sick of how cranky I am without coffee.) Once the chopping is done, these bars are super-quick to make. Feel free to use what you've got in your pantry: raisins, walnuts, dried blueberries. CM

Prep time: 20 minutes

Total time: 1 hour

Makes: 24 bars

½ cup (125 ml) packed brown sugar, packed

½ cup (125 ml) old-fashioned oats

⅓ cup (80 ml) oat flour
(if you don't have it, just throw ⅓ cup/80 ml old-fashioned oats in the food processor for a few minutes)

¼ cup (60 ml) flax meal

½ cup (125 ml) dried apricots, chopped quite fine

½ cup (125 ml) dried cranberries, chopped

⅓ cup (80 ml) pecans, finely chopped

¼ cup (60 ml) vegetable oil

¼ cup (60 ml) maple syrup

2 Tbsp (30 ml) brown rice syrup
(you could substitute corn syrup but I like the first option better)

Preheat the oven to 350°F (180°C). Line an 11- x 7-inch (28 x 18 cm) cake pan with parchment paper, leaving enough overhang to lift out the granola bars later.

Mix together the sugar, oats, oat flour, flax meal, apricots, cranberries and pecans. Make sure the fruits and nuts are evenly distributed.

In a large bowl, mix together the vegetable oil and both syrups.

Pour the dry ingredients on top of the wet and stir to combine thoroughly. Dump this granola mixture into the prepared pan. Use the back of a spoon to spread it out evenly.

Bake for 30 to 40 minutes. Keep an eye on the pan at the end, you want the mixture to just begin to brown. Let the pan cool for about 10 minutes before lifting out the parchment. Rest the parchment on the counter and let mixture cool completely. Cut into 1 ½- x 3-inch (4 x 7.5 cm) bars. Store in an airtight container for up to 1 week.

Sunflower Oat Balls

WHEN WE FIRST STARTED the SPC site, people immediately responded to recipes for pancakes, pastas and granola snacks. These dishes can often be quite sinful, so who wouldn't want to try a healthy alternative? Granola bars are oh-so-good (and easy to grab) but they are also oh-so-high in sugar. We tried to do something about that—and besides, kids love food in the shape of a ball, right? Okay, Ceri and I like that they're mini. LK

Prep time: 35 minutes
Total time: 1 hour 30 minutes
Makes: about 36

2 cups (500 ml) old-fashioned oats
1 cup (250 ml) unsweetened dried
    cranberries
½ cup (125 ml) dried blueberries
½ cup (125 ml) granola
½ cup (125 ml) shelled sunflower seeds
⅛ cup (25 ml) flax seeds
2 Tbsp (30 ml) chia powder (optional)
½ cup (125 ml) agave nectar (you can also
    use honey, but your snack will be
    sweeter)
½ cup (125 ml) sunflower butter
¼ cup (60 ml) brown sugar, packed

Preheat the oven to 350°F (180°C). Line a baking sheet with parchment paper.

Spread the oats out on another baking sheet and toast in the oven until lightly browned, 15 to 20 minutes.

In a large bowl, combine the toasted oats with the cranberries, blueberries, granola, sunflower seeds, flax seeds and chia powder and stir to mix. Set aside.

Mix together the agave nectar, sunflower butter and brown sugar in a medium-size saucepan over low heat. Stir continuously until the brown sugar is melted, about 3 minutes.

Remove the butter-sugar mixture from the heat and pour it over the oats and dried fruit. Stir until everything is completely combined. Let cool for a few minutes.

With moist hands, roll a teaspoonful of mixture in the palms of your hands. Create bite-size balls, roughly 1-inch (2.5 cm) in diameter, and place them on the prepared baking sheet. Place the tray in the refrigerator and allow the granola balls to harden for at least 1 hour. Store in an airtight container for up to 1 week.

The Benefits of Baking with Kids

WE KNOW. Cooking with the kids is like having a massage in the fast lane of a highway during rush hour. Okay, maybe not that bad, but the mess, oh, the mess. And yet studies consistently show that children who are involved in preparing a meal are more likely to eat it. To introduce children to the joys of cooking, we recommend having your children accompany you in the kitchen when you bake. Not only do the recipes have lots of fun components kids love (measuring, stirring, cracking eggs), baking is perfect for a weekend afternoon when you have more time. It's always best to begin with recipes that your children love, and what kid doesn't want to be part of a project that yields warm, gooey treats? (Healthy-ish, of course.) LK

Maple Corn Bread

ONE OF ESME'S BEST FRIENDS, Maude, brought corn bread to the park one day, and for weeks after Esme kept asking me to make it. I had a hunch that what she found so memorable about Maude's snack was the slick of maple syrup that had obviously been brushed onto the bread. I came up with this version, which is great with a bowl of soup at lunchtime, but the kids really love it when I cut a piece in half crossways and make a little jam sandwich out of it. CM

Prep time: 15 minutes
Total time: 40 minutes
Makes: 18 pieces

2 cups (500 ml) cornmeal
1 cup (250 ml) all-purpose flour
1 cup (250 ml) whole wheat flour
2 Tbsp (30 ml) baking powder
1 tsp (5 ml) baking soda
1 tsp (5 ml) salt
4 eggs
2 cups (500 ml) milk
1 ¼ cups (310 ml) unsweetened applesauce
½ cup (125 ml) + ¼ cup (60 ml) maple syrup
½ cup (125 ml) butter, melted

Preheat the oven to 450°F (230°C). Lightly grease a 9- x 13-inch (23 x 33 cm) baking pan.

In a large bowl, mix together the cornmeal, both flours, baking powder, baking soda and salt.

In another bowl, whisk together the eggs, milk, applesauce, ½ cup (125 ml) of maple syrup and the melted butter. Add the dry mixture to the wet and mix to combine well.

Pour the batter into the prepared pan and use the back of a spoon to smooth it down into the edges. Bake for 20 to 25 minutes until golden brown and a toothpick inserted in the center comes out clean.

Allow the bread to cool for a few minutes. Now use the toothpick to poke holes, maybe 11 or 12, all over the top. Take the remaining ¼ cup (60 ml) of maple syrup and either brush it overtop or spread it evenly with the back of a spoon. Allow to cool completely before cutting into pieces.

Zucchini Bread

'M FAIRLY ORGANIZED when it comes to having healthy food around for breakfast, lunch and dinner. But I confess: snacks are in my blind spot. That's right, my kids are the ones looking longingly at your kids' snacks at the park. Sorry. I'm trying! I like to bake something like this zucchini bread, which reminds me of my childhood on the west coast, where zucchini grows unstoppably, like a weed. And—bonus!—this recipe can supply snacks for at least four trips to the park. CM

Prep time: 20 minutes
Total time: 1 hour 20 minutes
Makes: 1 loaf (or 6 mini loaves)

1 ½ cups (375 ml) all-purpose flour
¾ cup (185 ml) whole wheat flour
¼ cup (60 ml) wheat bran
1 tsp (5 ml) salt
1 tsp (5 ml) baking powder
1 tsp (5 ml) baking soda
1 tsp (5 ml) ground cinnamon
½ tsp (2 ml) ground nutmeg
2 eggs
½ cup (125 ml) granulated sugar
½ cup (125 ml) Greek yogurt
¼ cup (60 ml) vegetable oil
2 tsp (10 ml) vanilla extract
2 cups (500 ml) grated zucchini
½ cup (125 ml) grated carrot
1 cup (250 ml) raisins
½ cup (125 ml) chopped dried apricots
½ cup (125 ml) chopped pecans

Preheat the oven to 350°F (180°C). Lightly grease a 9- x 5-inch (23 x 13 cm) loaf pan.

In a large bowl, whisk together both flours, the wheat bran, salt, baking powder, baking soda, cinnamon and nutmeg.

In another bowl, mix together the eggs, sugar, yogurt, oil and vanilla until well combined. Add the dry mixture to the wet and stir to combine well.

Stir in the zucchini, carrot, raisins, apricots and pecans until everything is evenly distributed throughout the batter.

Pour the batter into the prepared loaf pan. Bake for 50 to 60 minutes, or until a toothpick inserted in the center comes out clean. Cool in the pan for 15 minutes before turning the loaf out onto a rack to cool completely. Loaf will keep in an airtight container or wrapped in plastic wrap for 1 week.

Piña Colada Muffins

THESE MUFFINS ARE SUPER-MOIST, and the list of fun ingredients helps distract from the fact that they're also a really healthy snack. To get the best-tasting muffins, be sure to use very ripe bananas. Like all muffins, these freeze well. CM

Prep time: 20 minutes

Total time: 45 minutes

Makes: 12 muffins

2 eggs

1 ½ cups (375 ml) mashed ripe banana
    (about 3 bananas)

½ cup (125 ml) Greek yogurt

½ cup (125 ml) brown sugar, packed

1 tsp (5 ml) vanilla extract

1 cup (250 ml) all-purpose flour

1 cup (250 ml) whole wheat flour

1 tsp (5 ml) baking powder

½ tsp (2 ml) baking soda

½ tsp (2 ml) salt

½ tsp (2 ml) ground cardamom

¾ cup (185 ml) finely chopped
    fresh pineapple (be sure to
    drain it well)

½ cup (125 ml) shredded unsweetened
    coconut

Optional Topping

¼ cup (60 ml) shredded unsweetened
    coconut

¼ cup (60 ml) brown sugar, packed

Preheat the oven to 350°F (180°C). Lightly grease or line a muffin tin.

In a large bowl, mix together the eggs, banana, yogurt vanilla and sugar.

In another bowl, mix together the flours, baking powder, baking soda, salt and cardamom. Add the dry ingredients to the wet and stir to combine. Do not overmix. Stir in the pineapple and coconut.

Spoon the batter into the prepared muffin tin. Fill each muffin cup three-quarters full. If you want a little extra sweetness and crunch, mix together equal parts coconut and brown sugar and sprinkle over the batter.

Bake for 25 minutes, or until a toothpick inserted in the center comes out clean.

Orange Chocolate Mini Muffins

SCARLETT HAD AN ORANGE FIXATION for a while. I've had a chocolate addiction for most of my life. This is what we ended up with when we thought about muffins. (Oh, and we made them mini!) You are so welcome. **LK**

Prep time: 20 minutes

Total time: 45 minutes

Makes: 20 2-inch (5 cm) mini muffins

1 ¾ cups (435 ml) whole wheat
       pastry flour
½ cup (125 ml) cocoa powder
1 ½ tsp (7.5 ml) baking powder
½ tsp (2 ml) chia powder (optional)
¼ tsp (1 ml) salt
½ cup (125 ml) unsalted butter,
       room temperature
½ cup (125 ml) brown sugar, packed
2 large eggs
⅔ cup (160 ml) plain yogurt
½ cup (125 ml) orange juice (pulp-free)
1 tsp (5 ml) vanilla extract
½ cup (125 ml) mini milk chocolate chips

Preheat the oven to 350°F (180°C). Lightly grease or line a mini muffin tin.

In a medium-size bowl, whisk together the flour, cocoa powder, baking powder, chia powder and salt. Set aside.

Using an electric mixer, cream the butter with the sugar. Add the eggs, yogurt, orange juice and vanilla. Mix on low until combined. Slowly add the flour mixture to these wet ingredients. Once well mixed, stir in the chocolate chips.

Fill each muffin cup, leaving ¼ inch (0.5 cm) from the rim. Bake on the center rack for 25 to 30 minutes, or until a toothpick inserted into the center comes out clean. Let cool in the tin.

WHAT'S SO GREAT ABOUT CHIA? The teeny chia seed is a complete protein containing all nine amino acids essential to the body. Don't let its size fool you. Chia also offers a mountain of soluable fiber and omega-3 fatty acids. Black or white, the seeds are tasteless and odorless so are great over yogurt, cereals and in baking. If you're using chia oil keep in mind heat diminishes its nutritional benefits, so try it in salads and smoothies. **LK**

Whole Grain Blueberry Muffins

THE KIDS AND I were over at my friend Victoria's for a playdate one morning when she pointed out that our site didn't have a basic blueberry muffin recipe. So off I went to the kitchen to experiment. But thinking of Victoria's beautiful kids, I decided basic wouldn't cut it. These are the muffins—healthier, more delicious and so much more than basic—that I came up with. This recipe's so easy it's ideal for making with kids. CM

Prep time: 15 minutes
Total time: 35 minutes
Makes: 12 muffins

1 ¼ cups (310 ml) whole wheat flour
1 ¼ cups (310 ml) quick-cooking oats
¼ cup (60 ml) flax meal
1 tsp (5 ml) baking powder
½ tsp (2 ml) baking soda
½ tsp (2 ml) ground cinnamon
¼ tsp (1 ml) salt
1 cup (250 ml) applesauce
½ cup (125 ml) brown sugar, packed
½ cup (125 ml) buttermilk
    (or add 1 ½ tsp/7.5 ml of white
    vinegar to ½ cup/125 ml milk and
    let stand for 10 minutes)
2 Tbsp (30 ml) vegetable oil
1 egg
¾ cup (185 ml) blueberries
    (if you're using frozen, let them thaw
    before adding)

Preheat the oven to 375°F (190°C). Lightly grease or line a muffin tin.

In a large bowl, mix together the flour, oats, flax meal, baking powder, baking soda, cinnamon and salt.

In another bowl, mix together the applesauce, sugar, buttermilk, vegetable oil and egg.

Gently shake the dry ingredients into the wet, giving the mixture a stir every few shakes. Stir in the blueberries.

Pour the batter evenly into the muffin tin cups, filling only two-thirds of the way, and pop them in the oven for 20 minutes. They're done when they're firm and a toothpick inserted in the center comes out clean.

Wagamama Cookies

We're lucky to live over Wagamama Pastries, the best little café in Toronto. Honestly, we're in there almost every day, picking up coffees, grabbing a snack for the park and chatting with the other regulars. Julian and Esme have come to think of it as an extension of our own kitchen. When Laura and I were thinking of the ultimate chocolate chip cookie to include in this book it seemed silly to pretend that there's a better one than the Wagamama cookie, because there just isn't. Luckily, owners Miwa and John agreed to share their recipe with us. There must be some kind of magic in their kitchen, however, since these don't quite replicate the perfection of the ones at the café. Sorry, but for those you'll just have to go there yourself. CM

Prep time: 10 minutes
Total time: 20 minutes
Makes: 8 big cookies

⅔ cup (160 ml) butter, room temperature
¾ cup (185 ml) brown sugar, packed
1 ½ Tbsp (22 ml) brown rice syrup
    (you could sub in corn syrup)
1 tsp (5 ml) salt
½ tsp (2 ml) vanilla extract
1 egg
1 ½ cups (375 ml) all-purpose flour
1 tsp (2 ml) baking powder
1 tsp (2 ml) baking soda
1 cup (250 ml) rolled oats
¾ cup (185 ml) chocolate chips
    (I like semi-sweet but use
    what you've got!)
½ cup (125 ml) finely chopped walnuts
½ cup (125 ml) shredded unsweetened
    coconut

Preheat the oven to 350°F (180°C). Line a baking sheet with parchment paper.

In a large bowl, use an electric mixer to cream the butter and sugar until light and fluffy. Add the brown rice syrup and salt. Continue mixing and add the vanilla and then the egg.

In another bowl, sift together the flour, baking powder and baking soda.

Add the dry mixture to the wet in three additions, mixing as you go. Scrape down the edges of the bowl with a spatula in between each addition. Add the oats, chocolate chips, walnuts and coconut and mix until just combined.

Use an ice cream scoop or a ¼ cup (60 ml) measure to scoop the batter onto the prepared baking sheet.
Leave 1 inch (2.5 cm) between each cookie. Flatten each cookie to 1 inch (2.5 cm) thickness with the bottom of a measuring cup or the back of a spoon.

Bake for 10 minutes. Remove from the oven and allow the cookies to cool a bit before removing from the baking sheet to cool completely on a rack.

Cocoa Date Bars

ON A WINTER BREAK in Florida, I discovered these little date bars at a great organic market. They have an unexpected hit of cocoa in them, and I quickly became addicted, throwing them into our beach bag every day as a late-afternoon snack. (I also ate them as a late-night treat. Don't judge!) One especially peckish afternoon, as I performed micro-surgery to remove the two million grains of sand implanted in my bar, I vowed to replicate my beach obsession as soon as I returned to Toronto. Well, folks, here it is. Minus the sand. LK

Prep time: 10 minutes
Total time: 2 hours 10 minutes
Makes: about 20 little nibbles

½ cup (125 ml) sunflower seeds
½ cup (125 ml) sesame seeds,
    plus 2 Tbsp (30 ml) for topping
½ cup (125 ml) shredded unsweetened
    coconut
¼ cup (60 ml) dark cocoa
1 ½ cups (375 ml) pitted and roughly
    chopped dried Medjool dates
½ cup (125 ml) raisins
1 tsp (5 ml) coconut oil

Line a small baking sheet with parchment paper, leaving a 1-inch (2.5 cm) overhang at the edges.

Place the sunflower and ½ cup (125 ml) of sesame seeds in a food processor and process until they have the consistency of breadcrumbs. Add the coconut and cocoa, and mix well.

Add the dates, raisins and coconut oil and process until fully combined. (Don't worry about the sticky dates and raisins causing the mixture to form a ball. Just continue to work it until the seeds and coconut are evenly distributed throughout the mixture.)

Using damp hands, remove the date mixture from the processor and press it out to a 1-inch (2.5 cm) thick rectangle on the prepared baking sheet. Sprinkle the top of the dates with the 2 Tbsp (30 ml) sesame seeds and lightly press them into the mix.

Place the baking sheet in the refrigerator for at least 2 hours. Remove the baking sheet from the refrigerator. You want to keep these sweet babies small so cut them into 1-inch (2.5 cm) squares. Store in an airtight container for up to 2 weeks.

Applewich
with all the Trimmings

THIS IS AN ODE TO MY BEAUTIFUL, warm, funny and infinitely loving mother, who prepared this easy snack for me as a kid over and over and over again. I swear the woman didn't have a single other snack idea in her arsenal, and I couldn't have cared less. Below you'll find our favorite fillings, but you could use carob chips, currants, dried blueberries, slivered almonds . . . LK

Prep time: 5 minutes

Total time: 10 minutes

Makes: 2 servings

2 Granny Smith apples,
   cored and cut crosswise

1 tsp (5 ml) fresh lemon or orange juice

¼ cup (60 ml) almond butter

2 Tbsp (30 ml) sunflower seeds

2 Tbsp (30 ml) shredded unsweetened
   coconut

1 Tbsp (15 ml) flax seeds

2 Tbsp (30 ml) unsweetened
   dried cranberries

Cut the apple into crosswise slices thick enough to hold the toppings and brush them with lemon or orange juice to keep them from turning brown, especially if you're packing these snacks for later.

Working with pairs, lay the apple slices out on a flat surface. Spread a slice with almond butter and then sprinkle with sunflower seeds, coconut, flax seeds or cranberries as desired. Place another slice on top and lightly press down to make a sandwich. Serve on a plate or pack in an airtight container for on-the-go eating.

WHAT'S SO GREAT ABOUT FLAX? The small but mighty flax seed is off-the-charts in omega-3s, which means you can count on it for cardio health protection and for the way it improves ratios of LDL (bad) to HDL (good) cholesterol levels. But one of its most powerful traits is the way its high fiber content slows down digestion, improving the intestinal absorption of nutrients consumed along with it. The simplest way to buy flax is ground. Add flax meal to smoothies, hot oatmeal and any kind of baking. It adds the subtlest nutty flavor to recipes. Just be sure to store flax meal in the refrigerator once you've opened the package. CM

Roasted Pumpkin Seeds

AFTER SPENDING MOST MORNINGS of her life watching me shovel Greek yogurt mixed with various seeds and currants into my mouth, Scarlett has officially been brainwashed. She loves roasted seeds, and pumpkin are her favorite. That's why I try to have an abundance of both savory and sweet seeds at our disposal. Hopefully, she won't also acquire my habit of sneaking a handful of chocolate-covered almonds before bed. Forget I mentioned that. **LK**

Prep time: 10 minutes
Total time: 55 minutes
Makes: 2 cups (500 ml) per option

Sweet

2 cups (500 ml) raw whole pumpkin seeds
1 Tbsp (15 ml) maple syrup
2 tsp (10 ml) olive oil
1 tsp (5 ml) brown sugar
1 tsp (5 ml) ground cinnamon

Preheat the oven to 300°F (150°C). Line a baking sheet with parchment paper.

Toss the seeds in a bowl with the maple syrup, oil, sugar and cinnamon. Spread the seeds over the baking sheet in a single layer and bake for 45 minutes or until golden brown, stirring occasionally to avoid burning.

Savory

2 cups (500 ml) raw whole pumpkin seeds
2 tsp (10 ml) olive oil
1 tsp (5 ml) chili powder
½ tsp (2 ml) garlic powder

Preheat the oven to 300°F (150°C). Line a baking sheet with parchment paper.

Toss the seeds in a bowl with the oil, chili powder and garlic powder. Spread the seeds over the baking sheet in a single layer and bake for 45 minutes or until golden brown, stirring occasionally to avoid burning.

Roasted Chickpeas

RICH IN FIBER AND CALCIUM as well as vitamins A, C and K, chickpeas (also known as garbanzo beans) are a very nutritious but not always easy snack choice. But then Scarlett and I stumbled upon a package of roasted chickpeas laden with cinnamon. She fell in love with their sweet flavor, and I couldn't resist their ease. Feel free to toss a container of these babies into a backpack or purse—places hummus would not dare venture. **LK**

Prep time: 10 minutes
Total time: 1 hour
Makes: about 2 cups (500 ml)

1 can (15 oz/443 ml) chickpeas, drained and rinsed
¼ cup (60ml) maple syrup
1 tsp (5 ml) coconut oil
½ tsp (2 ml) vanilla extract
2 tsp (10 ml) ground cinnamon
Ground allspice

Preheat the oven to 375°F (190°C). Line a baking sheet with parchment paper.

Toss the chickpeas in a bowl with the maple syrup, oil and vanilla, and add the cinnamon and a pinch of allspice. Mix well.

Spread the chickpeas over the prepared baking sheet in a single layer. Bake, stirring occasionally, for about 40 minutes, or until golden brown and crunchy outside.

Shakshuka

Asparagus and Tomato Frittata

Sweet Corn Tostada

ABC Quesadilla

Kale and Red Pepper Cheesey Calzone

Lemon Linguini

Pumpkin and Sage Cannelloni

Chicken Chili Tacos

Apple Chicken Curry

OMG Chicken Parm

Herbed Chicken Tray Bake

Mini Meatloaves

Tilapia Tacos with Fresh Lime

Shrimp with Bacon and Polenta

Crunchy Baked Fish and Chips

Salmon Dinner Salad

Salmon Cakes

Grilled Shrimp Salad

Tuna Steaks over Soba Noodles

Rosemary Dijon Rack of Lamb

Ginger Pork over Pasta

Spaghetti and Meatballs

Beef Lettuce Wraps

Nana Molly's Stuffed Artichokes

Pears with Goat Cheese and Cranberries

Glazed Green Vegetables

Roasted Vegetables

Butternut Squash and Apple Purée

Beet Slaw

Couscous Pilaf

Farro and Roasted Vegetables

Lentil Salad

Currant Apricot Rice

dinner

DINNER OUTSIDE

Watermelon Lemonade

Grape Salsa

Gruyère and Herb Turkey Burgers

Chicken and Peach Skewers

Sweet Corn and Green Bean Salad

Watermelon Salad

Shakshuka

SHAKSHUKA IS THE KIND OF RECIPE that starts fights in the comments section of food blogs. *It's Tunisian. No, it's Libyan! It's absolutely Israeli. Never add feta. My mother always uses feta!* So, apologies in advance. I'm quite sure my version of this zesty tomato sauce topped with poached eggs is not traditional. But it is so delicious, it takes about half an hour to make and I bet you have all the ingredients in your kitchen right now. My kids love it and not just because it's fun to say. But it's really fun to say. *Shakshuka!* CM

Prep time: 5 minutes
Total time: 30-35 minutes
Makes: 4 servings

2 Tbsp (30 ml) olive oil
1 onion, diced quite fine
3 or 4 cloves garlic, minced
1 tsp (5 ml) paprika
½ tsp (2 ml) ground cumin
Chili flakes (optional)
1 can (28 oz/796 ml) whole tomatoes
1 Tbsp (15 ml) tomato paste
Salt and pepper
6 eggs
¼ cup (60 ml) crumbled feta
Handful of chopped basil or parsley

Heat the olive oil in a large, high-sided frying pan over medium heat. Add the onion and garlic and let them become really soft and begin to brown. Now add the paprika, cumin and a pinch of chili flakes and stir. Let the spices cook for about 3 minutes. Pour the tomatoes and the tomato paste in there and use a potato masher to gently break them up. Allow the sauce to simmer away for about 20 minutes, until it becomes quite thick. Taste and add salt and pepper accordingly.

Use the back of a wooden spoon to spread the sauce evenly across the frying pan. Now gently crack the eggs over the tomato sauce. I usually place five in a circle around the pan and one in the center. Cook them for 6 or 7 minutes. You can cover it all for the last minute if you like the tops of your eggs quite set. Crumble the feta and basil or parsley overtop.

Shimmy a big serving spoon under each egg to scoop them out of the pan. Serve with crusty bread and some steamed vegetables.

Asparagus and Tomato Frittata

'M PROUD TO SAY this is the first meal Scarlett cooked on her own. (I did the broiling.) I think the reason she felt so confident throwing this recipe together for us was because she'd seen me do it so many times before. **LK**

Prep time: 10 minutes

Total time: 25 minutes

Makes: 4 servings

1 Tbsp (15 ml) unsalted butter

¼ cup (60 ml) chopped white onion

1 ½ cups (375 ml) trimmed and chopped
    asparagus

3 cloves garlic, minced

8 eggs

¼ cup (60 ml) milk

Salt and pepper

¼ cup (60 ml) grated Parmesan cheese

7 cherry tomatoes, halved

2 Tbsp (30 ml) shredded fontina cheese

In a 9- or 10-inch (23 or 25 cm) nonstick, ovenproof frying pan, melt the butter over medium heat. Add the onion, asparagus and garlic and cook until the asparagus is tender-crisp, about 5 minutes.

In a bowl, whisk the eggs with the milk plus salt and pepper to taste. Add the Parmesan cheese and stir to combine. Pour the eggs into the asparagus mixture. Cover and cook over medium-low heat until the bottom begins to firm up, 8 to 10 minutes. Scatter the tomato halves into the egg mixture. Cook for 3 to 5 more minutes, or until the sides are firm but the top is slightly runny. Sprinkle with fontina cheese.

Turn the broiler on low and place the frying pan on the top rack of the oven. Broil the frittata until the edges are golden, the egg is set and the cheese is melted, about 1 minute. Remove from broiler and allow to cool for a few minutes before slicing and serving.

Sweet Corn Tostada

I MADE THIS DISH UP one summer night when our day's activities had left barely enough time to prep dinner, let alone eat it. With bedtime pressing down on us, my husband bet me I couldn't get dinner on the table in 20 minutes. He lost, and we ate well. LK

Prep time: 10 minutes
Total time: 20 minutes
Makes: 4 servings

1 can (14 oz/398 ml) no-salt-added black beans,
    drained and rinsed
¼ cup (60 ml) olive oil
Juice of 1 lime
¼ cup (60 ml) chopped cilantro, plus
    ¼ cup (60 ml) for garnish
1 clove garlic, roughly chopped
Salt
1 ear of corn, or 1 cup (250 ml) frozen kernels
½ head iceberg lettuce, shredded
¾ cup (185 ml) shaved Monterey Jack cheese
½ cup (125 ml) sour cream
8 corn tortillas

Place the beans, oil, lime juice, ¼ cup (60 ml) cilantro, garlic and a pinch of salt in a food processor. Blend until the mixture has a smooth consistency, similar to hummus. Remove from the food processor and spoon into a small bowl. Set aside.

Meanwhile, bring a large pot of unsalted water to a boil. Place the ear of corn in the pot and cook, covered, for 3 to 4 minutes. Remove from the water and let cool for a few minutes. Scrape the kernels into a bowl. Set aside. If using frozen corn, cook according to package directions.

Preheat the oven to 300°F (150°C)

Wrap your tortillas in a damp dish towel and place them in a medium-size casserole dish. Cover the dish with its lid or some aluminum foil. Place the dish with the tortillas in the oven for about 10 minutes. Arrange a warm tortilla on a plate and layer with black bean mixture, lettuce, cheese and corn. Go ahead and free-style this dish with additional toppings like chopped bell peppers and tomatoes and slices of avocado. Serve with the remaining cilantro and sour cream.

Must Meat Make the Meal?

WHAT DEFINES DINNER? Like most of us, I grew up with an unequivocal answer: meat and two veg. But the meals we prepare when our kids are small are a chance to shake things up. One notion we embrace is "flexitariansim"—making at least one day each week meatless. The health benefits of limiting your meat intake are undeniable. Multiple studies show that it reduces the risk for cancer, heart disease, diabetes and obesity. Of course, you have to eat good things in place of meat, like whole grains, fruits and vegetables. And it can be tough for some adults to make the switch, which is why introducing our kids to meatless meals is so important. When you think of the variety of vegetables, fruits and grains available to us compared to the few types of meat we eat, going "flexitarian" actually opens the doors to many more mealtime options. But to begin with, just make friends with a handful of vegetarian recipes and you'll be on your way. CM

ABC Quesadilla

The name of this recipe comes from the big doses of vitamins A, B and C it packs. Whenever I want my kids to try something new, I like to be sure I'm also serving something they love. This meal was literally a way for me to sandwich spinach and black beans between cheese and tortillas. My system doesn't always work—I could dip rapini in chocolate and my kids still wouldn't eat it—but in this case it did. CM

Prep time: 15 minutes
Total time: 25 minutes
Makes: 4 servings

1 can (15 oz/443 ml) black beans
2 Tbsp (30 ml) olive oil
1 onion, finely chopped
2 cloves garlic, minced
½ tsp (2 ml) ground cumin
½ tsp (2 ml) chili powder
1 bunch fresh baby spinach
1 medium tomato, diced
1 ½ cups (375 ml) shredded
    cheddar cheese
4 8-inch (20 cm) flax tortillas
    (or corn or whole wheat if that's
    what you've got handy)

Rinse the black beans well in a sieve. Set aside.

Heat 1 Tbsp (15 ml) of the olive oil in a large frying pan over medium heat. Add the onion and garlic and sauté until soft, 3 to 5 minutes. Add the cumin and chili powder, stir and cook for another minute. Add the beans. Using the back of a fork or a potato masher, break up the beans until about half of them are mashed. Cook the beans for a few minutes, stirring frequently so they don't stick. Remove from the heat and set aside.

Wash and dry the spinach, trim the stalks and discard, then coarsely chop the leaves. In another pan, drizzle a tiny bit of olive oil and warm it over medium heat. Add the spinach and stir. Allow it to wilt and soften, 3 to 5 minutes. Remove from the heat. As you're taking the spinach out of the pan, press it against the edge to drain.

Heat a drizzle of olive oil in a large clean frying pan over medium-high heat. Lay the first tortilla in the frying pan. Spread half the black bean mixture on the tortilla, then half the spinach, half the tomato and half the cheese. Place a second tortilla on top. Press something on top to flatten the quesadilla. I've used a small cast-iron pan in the past, or sometimes I'll use a small plate with a big can of chickpeas on top to add weight. Cook for 3 or 4 minutes and then remove the weight. Use a spatula under the quesadilla—your hand pressing gently down on top—to flip it over. Cook on the other side for another 3 or 4 minutes with the weight on top again. Remove from the heat and place on a cutting board. Cut, pizza-style, into 6 or 8 pieces.

Repeat with the remaining ingredients. Serve with sour cream or plain yogurt, salsa, avocado and a big scoop of brown rice.

WHAT'S SO GREAT ABOUT BLACK BEANS? When looking for meat alternatives, black beans make an excellent case for themselves. One cup (250 ml) of cooked black beans boasts about ½ oz (15 g) of protein (30% of an adult's daily requirement) as well as ½ oz (15 g) of fiber (over 60% of what you need each day). Black beans can also brag about the major iron, vitamin B1 and folates they provide—a nutritional combination that's effective in lowering cholesterol levels, improving cardiovascular health and regulating blood sugar levels. Canned black beans make life easy (there's no loss in nutrition) but look for brands that use BPA-free tins. CM

Kale and Red Pepper Cheesey Calzone

PIZZA WAS AN EASY DISH for Scarlett and me when we began cooking together. Her three-year-old hands fit perfectly around the rolling pin handles. On a whim, I decided to switch up our regular pizza dish for these kale pockets. We love to freeze and reheat them for those nights when the idea of making dinner feels like climbing Everest. LK

Prep time: 1 hour

Total time: 1 hour 50 minutes

Makes: 4–6 servings

1 lb (450 g) store-bought whole wheat
     pizza dough
3 Tbsp (45 ml) grapeseed oil
½ cup (125 ml) chopped onion
1 red bell pepper, chopped
Salt
2 cloves garlic, minced
2 cups (500 ml) frozen chopped kale
     (you can also use spinach)
2 balls (each 12 oz/340 g) mozzarella cheese
1 cup (250 ml) tomato sauce
     (see Quickie Red Sauce on page 145),
     plus extra for dipping
½ cup (125 ml) grated Parmesan cheese

Dust a bowl with flour and place the pizza dough in it. Dust the top of the dough with more flour and then cover with a damp dish towel. Allow the dough to stand in the bowl at room temperature for about 1 hour until it has doubled in size.

Preheat the oven to 450°F (230°C) and put the oven rack into its lowest position. Cover a large baking sheet with parchment paper.

In a large frying pan, heat 2 Tbsp (30 ml) of the grapeseed oil over medium heat. Add the onion, red pepper and a sprinkling of salt and cook until the onion begins to brown and the pepper is beginning to soften but is still a bit crisp, 8 to 10 minutes. Add the garlic and cook until fragrant, another minute or two. Add the frozen kale and stir until it has wilted and softened, 3 to 4 minutes.

Meanwhile, tear the cheese into small pieces. On a floured surface, roll out the pizza dough with a lightly floured rolling pin until it's about a ¼-inch (0.5 cm) thick rectangle. Cut the dough into four square-ish pieces.

Working with one piece of dough at a time, spoon 2 Tbsp (30 ml) of the tomato sauce onto the dough and then place a heaping tablespoon (25 ml) or even a bit more of the kale and pepper mixture on a diagonal toward one corner of the square. Add a few pieces of mozzarella and sprinkle with Parmesan cheese. Lifting the bottom right corner, fold the dough toward the top left corner. Pinch the edges of the calzone together, pulling the dough upward to close. Brush the top surface of the calzone with the remaining 1 Tbsp (15 ml) oil and carefully slice three steam vents into the top.

Transfer to the prepared baking sheet and bake in the oven until golden brown, about 15 minutes. Cool for a few minutes and then serve with a side of warm tomato sauce for dipping.

Lemon Linguini

I F I ASK MY KIDS what they want for dinner, the answer is always the same: noodles! And of all the noodles they ask for, cheesey noodles top the list. In an effort to shake things up, I started working this lemony pasta dish into our regular rotation. It still has all the cozy qualities you want in a comfort dish but the lemon manages to lighten it up. You could serve this with a side of steamed asparagus or peas but it could also be a side itself. CM

Prep time: 10 minutes
Total time: 20 minutes
Makes: 4 main servings or
6 side servings

1 package (1 lb/450 g) linguini or spaghetti
½-⅔ cup (125-160 ml) lemon juice
(about 2 good-sized lemons)
1 Tbsp (15 ml) lemon zest
6 Tbsp (90 ml) olive oil
2 cups (500 ml) grated Parmesan cheese
Handful of basil, washed and
sliced into strips
Salt and pepper

Cook the pasta according to the package instructions. Meanwhile, whisk together the lemon juice and zest, oil and 1 ½ cups (375 ml) of the cheese. You'll have quite a gloopy mixture.

Scoop out ½ cup (125 ml) of the pasta cooking water and set it aside, then drain the noodles. Put the pasta back in the cooking pot. Pour the lemon mixture over the pasta and toss well until all the noodles are coated. Add a splash of your reserved pasta water if you need to loosen up the dish. Now add the basil and toss again. Add salt and pepper to taste.

Serve up the pasta and sprinkle the last of the cheese overtop.

Chores and Manners for Peace

WE ALL HAVE A VISION of what family meals should look like. Happy times at the table, sharing the details of our days over lovingly prepared food. Too often our reality—bickering siblings on one side of the table and badgering parents on the other—leaves everyone feeling more depleted than nourished. Enter chores and manners. I know, I know, but stick with me here. Central to SPC's philosophy is the belief that involving kids in the food they eat might be harder, slower, messier in the beginning but is so worth the investment. The same approach might be applied to the whole world of the table. A kid who sets the table or washes the dishes is less likely to see you as his short-order cook. And a child who knows to place a napkin in her lap or use her cutlery properly will not only be a more pleasant dining companion for you, but she will have more social confidence when she's out in the world on her own. And yes, you're going to have to remind them about three hundred and fifty million times before they do these things on their own but what part of parenting isn't like that? The trickiest part? You've got to lead by example. So put down the phone, turn off the TV, sit up straight, elbows off the table . . . actually, I've never understood that one. CM

Pumpkin and Sage Cannelloni

WHEN SCARLETT TURNED SIX, she shocked me by announcing she didn't want a birthday party. Instead she asked for a dinner party with some close friends and family, and she requested that cheesey shells be on the menu. Stuck for a recipe, I asked my brother's wife, Amanda, for help. She created this dish for me. Since Scarlett's birthday is in the fall, Amanda added some roasted pumpkin as well as a béchamel sauce to take this cheesey dish right over the top. It does take some time to prepare (and a lot of pots—goodness, the pots that need washing) but Amanda gave me some great time-saving tips as well as a recipe for an alternative red sauce. Let's just be real—unless you're six, you can't always afford to go over the top. LK

Prep time: 45 minutes
Total time: 1 hour 30 minutes
Makes: 6–8 servings

Pumpkin Cannelloni

4 cups (1 L) pumpkin, peeled and diced
¼ cup (60 ml) extra virgin olive oil
1 tsp (5 ml) salt
½ tsp (2 ml) pepper
2 Tbsp (30 ml) butter
1 medium shallot, finely minced
2 large cloves garlic, finely minced
½ cup (125 ml) low-sodium chicken
    or vegetable stock
8 sage leaves, finely sliced
1 whole nutmeg, finely grated
1 cup (250 ml) ricotta cheese
1 cup (250 ml) mascarpone cheese, softened
½ cup (125 ml) grated pecorino Romano,
    plus more for baking
1 large egg
¼ cup (60 ml) finely chopped walnuts,
    lightly toasted
14 cannelloni tubes

Quickie Red Sauce

2 Tbsp (30 ml) olive oil
1 small onion, finely chopped
2 large cloves garlic, minced
1 small carrot, peeled and grated
¼ cup (60 ml) white wine
1 can (28 oz/796 ml) whole tomatoes
3 Tbsp (45 ml) thyme leaves, roughly chopped
Salt and pepper

Traditional Béchamel

3 cups (750 ml) milk
1 medium onion, halved
2 large cloves garlic
4 whole cloves
1 bay leaf
1 tsp (5 ml) salt
White pepper
6 Tbsp (90 ml) butter
6 Tbsp (90 ml) all-purpose flour
1 whole nutmeg, finely grated

See overleaf for preparation

Preheat the oven to 450°F (230°C). Grease a 9- x 13- inch glass or ceramic baking dish.

Toss the diced pumpkin with just enough olive oil to barely coat it. Sprinkle with salt and pepper. Throw it onto a baking sheet and roast until lightly browned, about 40 minutes. Remove the pumpkin from the oven and set aside. Reduce the oven temperature to 350°F (180°C).

While the pumpkin is roasting, you can make the sauce.

For the red sauce, heat the olive oil in a frying pan over medium heat. Sauté the onion, garlic and carrot until lightly browned. Deglaze the pan by adding the white wine and scraping the bottom of the pan with a wooden spoon to dislodge any tasty bits. Add the tomatoes, thyme and salt and pepper to taste. Simmer on low heat for 10 to 15 minutes, stirring occasionally. Using an immersion blender, blend to desired consistency.

For the béchamel sauce, bring the milk, onion, garlic, cloves, bay leaf, salt and pepper to a simmer over medium heat in a heavy-bottomed saucepan, stirring as it comes to a simmer. Cover and reduce the heat to low for 5 minutes, stirring occasionally. Remove from the heat and allow the mixture to steep for about 5 minutes. Pour the milk through a fine mesh strainer into a bowl.

Melt the butter in a frying pan over medium heat. Add the flour and cook until it's a light tan color, stirring constantly. Add the strained milk and cook until thickened to a thin, gravy-like consistency, whisking constantly. Stir in the nutmeg and taste to check if you need more salt or pepper.

For the pumpkin filling, melt the 2 Tbsp (30 ml) butter in a saucepan over medium-low heat. Add the shallot and garlic and cook until caramelized. Toss these into the food processor with the roasted pumpkin, stock, sage and nutmeg. Process until smooth. Transfer the mixture to a bowl and stir in the cheeses, egg and walnuts. Taste to check the seasoning. You may want to add a bit more salt and pepper.

Fill a piping bag or plastic storage bag with the cheese mixture and pipe it into the cannelloni shells. Pour half the sauce into the glass baking dish then lay the stuffed cannelloni on top. Pour the remaining sauce over the cannelloni and sprinkle with extra pecorino Romano cheese.

Bake for about 45 minutes or until it's bubbly and the cheese has browned a bit on top. Remove from the oven and serve.

TIME-SAVING ALERT You can take a few shortcuts for this dish. For instance, use canned pumpkin so you can skip the roasting step and just sauté the shallot and garlic in butter and then jump to the food processor step. To make the piping easier, place the filling in a piping bag and refrigerate overnight or even just a few hours. Also, try using pregrated pecorino Romano cheese and prepared red sauce.

Chicken Chili Tacos

THIS DISH IS AN SPC FAVORITE that got a new spin from my sister-in-law, Amanda, who is as passionate about cooking as she is about a good taco. I can't stress enough how delicious and easy this dish is. I use it a lot for casual entertaining and I've never had a nose turned up at it. And believe me, this dish has been placed in front of some pretty picky noses. LK

Prep time: 10 minutes
Total time: 6 hours 10 minutes
Makes: 4 servings

6 boneless, skinless chicken thighs
1 ½ cups (375 ml) prepared pico de gallo
    or salsa
¼ cup (60 ml) fresh lime juice
    (about 1 ½ limes)
2 tsp (10 ml) cumin seeds, lightly toasted
¼ cup (60 ml) chopped fresh cilantro
12 taco shells (crisp or soft/flour or corn)

Place the chicken, pico de gallo or salsa, lime juice and cumin seeds in a slow cooker and stir to combine. Cover and cook on low for 6 hours. (You can cook on high for 3 hours.)

Allow to cool a bit. Scoop the chicken out with a big slotted spoon and place it in a large bowl. Use two forks to pull the meat apart. The chicken will shred easily. Stir in some cooking juices from the pot and add the cilantro.

Place the shredded chicken, your taco shells and desired fixings on the table and let everyone put together their own perfect taco.

Serving Suggestions
Sour cream
Guacamole
Pico de gallo or salsa
Shredded lettuce (or try arugula, cabbage, baby spinach)
Shredded cheese such as Monterey Jack or cheddar
    or try crumbled goat cheese for a flavor change

Apple Chicken Curry

THIS MILD AND SWEET curry is a great way to introduce a little spice to risk-averse eaters. And one pot for the rice plus one pot for the curry equals a speedy cleanup. CM

Prep time: 15 minutes
Total time: 30 minutes
Makes: 4 servings

1 cup (250 ml) brown basmati rice
Olive oil or butter
2 Tbsp (30 ml) vegetable oil
2 boneless, skinless chicken thighs,
    cut into bite-size pieces
1 onion, diced
2 cloves garlic, minced
1–2 tsp (5–10 ml) curry powder or paste
    (strength according to taste)
⅔ cup (160 ml) coconut milk
⅔ cup (160 ml) low-sodium
    chicken stock
1 tsp (5 ml) soy sauce
1 large firm-fleshed apple like
    Granny Smith or Gala, peeled, cored
    and sliced into ½-inch (1 cm) wedges
1 cup (250 ml) frozen peas
Plain yogurt to garnish

Pour 2 cups (500 ml) of water into a small pot with the basmati rice and the tiniest drop of olive oil or smidge of butter and then put a lid on it. Bring it to a boil and then reduce the heat so the rice simmers away for about 20 minutes. Try not to take the lid off too often to check but do turn the heat off just before all the water has been absorbed. As long as you keep the lid on the pot, the rice will stay hot and not dry out.

Meanwhile, warm up the vegetable oil in a large, high-sided frying pan over medium-high heat. Add the chicken and sauté until it just begins to brown. You may need to work in batches if the pan is becoming too crowded. Now add the onion and let it soften for about 5 minutes. Add the garlic and the curry powder or paste, stir everything together and cook for another minute.

Pour in the coconut milk, stock and soy sauce and stir. Add the apple slices and simmer for about 5 minutes. Toss in the peas and let them warm up for another minute. I always pluck out a piece of chicken at this point and cut into it to be sure it's completely cooked.

Place a scoop of rice in a bowl and top it with a ladleful or two of curry. Garnish with a dollop of plain yogurt and dinner is ready.

WHAT'S SO GREAT ABOUT LEEKS? Like all the members of the allium vegetable family—garlic, onions—leeks are powerful promoters of cardiovascular health. So why not sub them for onions in a recipe? As well as introducing a milder flavor to dishes, leeks deliver a hefty dose of immune-boosting vitamins A and C. By stimulating the growth of healthy bacteria in the lower intestines, leeks also improve what doctors and nutritionists so charmingly refer to as "gut health." CM

OMG Chicken Parm

My friend Natalee Caple and her twins, Moey and Casey, are frequent contributors to SPC. They shared this dinner with us early on, and it became one of the most popular posts we've ever published. I don't know why I even bother to write up the recipe the way I have since you should always, always double it. CM

Prep time: 25 minutes
Total time: 50 minutes
Makes: 8 pieces

2 Tbsp (30 ml) olive oil
2 cloves garlic, minced
1 can (28 oz/796 ml) whole plum tomatoes
2 Tbsp (30 ml) red wine vinegar
Salt and pepper
1–2 tsp (5–10 ml) dried herbs
    (any combination of basil,
    oregano and parsley)
4 boneless, skinless chicken breasts
1 ½ cups (375 ml) panko breadcrumbs
    or traditional dried breadcrumbs
1 cup (250 ml) milk
Big handful of fresh basil leaves
1 ½ cups (375 ml) grated
    Parmesan cheese

Warm up 1 Tbsp (15 ml) of the olive oil over medium heat in a good-sized pot. Sauté the garlic for just a couple of minutes before adding the tomatoes and vinegar. You can use the back of a wooden spoon to break them up but lately I've been using a potato masher and it works really well. (Just go slow so the tomatoes don't splash up on your clothes!) Let the tomato sauce simmer away for about 20 minutes. In the last few minutes, add salt and pepper to taste and the dried herbs.

Meanwhile, prepare the chicken. With a sharp chef's knife, slice the chicken breasts in half horizontally so you end up with 8 very thin pieces. Preheat the oven to 350°F (180°C).

Season the breadcrumbs with a bit of salt and pepper and spread them out on a plate. Pour the milk into a shallow bowl. Dip each piece of chicken in the milk, dredge it in the breadcrumbs, then set it aside on a clean plate.

In a large frying pan, add the remaining 1 Tbsp (15 ml) of olive oil and brown the chicken pieces over medium heat. Don't worry about cooking the meat through, you're just building a little color and flavor here. Work in batches so the pan is not crowded. Place the browned chicken pieces in a single layer in a casserole dish or roasting pan (don't worry if there is a bit of overlap of chicken pieces).

Cover the chicken with the tomato sauce, scatter a layer of fresh basil leaves across the sauce and top the whole thing with the cheese.

Bake in the oven for 15 minutes before increasing the temperature to 400°F (200°C) for another 10 minutes. Cut into a piece of chicken just to be sure it's cooked through. Chicken Parm is particularly good served with egg noodles.

Herbed Chicken Tray Bake

DON'T YOU ALWAYS CHECK IN with other parents to see what they're having for dinner? It's one of the things hanging over us all—damned dinner needs to be made again—so I do a survey of what everyone else is making to get my own juices flowing. One afternoon I asked a friend, and this dish was her answer. Well, not exactly. This is the SPC version of a dish she quickly rattled off to me, in between interruptions from our children and before she had to run off. That's the other thing about parents, we never get to finish a conversation. So, since I likely didn't get the chance to say it at the time, thank you, Gina. LK

Prep time: 20 minutes
Total time: 1 hour
Makes: 4–6 servings

¼ cup (60 ml) olive oil
Juice of 1 lemon
3 Tbsp (45 ml) chopped fresh oregano
Salt and pepper
4 chicken wings
2 boneless, skinless chicken breasts
2 boneless, skinless chicken thighs
3–4 lb (1.5–1.8 kg) red potatoes, halved
1 yellow zucchini, chopped
1 green zucchini, chopped
1 red onion, quartered
6 cloves garlic, peeled
32 cherry tomatoes, on or off the vine

Preheat the oven to 400°F (200°C). Spray a large rimmed baking tray with cooking spray.

In a small bowl, whisk together the oil, lemon juice, oregano and salt and pepper to taste.

In a medium bowl, toss the chicken with half the dressing. You can allow the chicken to marinate in the refrigerator for more intense flavor (anywhere from 1 to 3 hours) but it's also great if you use it right away.

In a separate large bowl, coat the potatoes, zucchinis and onion with the remaining half of the dressing. Scatter the vegetables and garlic on the prepared baking tray. Arrange the chicken on the tray as well.

Bake in the oven for 15 minutes. Take out the baking tray and scatter the cherry tomatoes across the top of the vegetables. Return to oven and bake for another 15 to 20 minutes, until the chicken is cooked through and the vegetables are tender.

Plate appropriate portions for family members (make mine big, please) from the tray and serve immediately.

Mini Meatloaves

BATCH COOKING IS ONE OF those amazing life-saving tricks that you try once and then never look back. I can't say that my freezer is always full of homemade goodness, but when I know we've got a crazy week coming up I like to spend some time on a Sunday whipping up a double batch of something that will ease the dinner-time pain. Like these little babies. They've got all the yummy appeal of a traditional meatloaf but on a kid-friendly scale. And I like that you only have to pull out as many as you need on any given night. CM

Prep time: 15 minutes
Total time: 55 minutes
Makes: 6 mini loaves

1 Tbsp (15 ml) olive oil
⅓ cup (80 ml) finely chopped onion
     (about ½ medium onion)
⅓ cup (80 ml) finely chopped celery
⅓ cup (80 ml) finely diced carrot
1 tsp (5 ml) fennel seeds
1 ½ lb (680 g) ground turkey
½ cup (125 ml) rolled oats
¼ cup (60 ml) grated Parmesan cheese
1 egg, whisked
¼ cup (60 ml) + 2 Tbsp (30 ml) ketchup
1 tsp (5 ml) Worcestershire sauce

Preheat the oven to 375°F (190°C). Warm the olive oil in a frying pan over medium heat. Add the onion, celery, carrot and fennel seeds and allow them to just start to soften, 3 to 5 minutes. Remove from the heat and let cool.

In a large mixing bowl, place the turkey, oats, Parmesan cheese, whisked egg, ¼ cup (60 ml) ketchup and the sautéed vegetables and and mix to combine well. You can use a wooden spoon but the best tools for this job are your hands. Remember to take your rings off! Really squish the mixture together—each bite should have a morsel of each ingredient. Okay, now wash your hands really well.

Using a ⅓ cup (80 ml) measure, scoop up the mixture and put it in a 6-cup muffin tin. In a small bowl, combine the 2 Tbsp (30 ml) of ketchup with the Worcestershire sauce. Use a spoon to smear a bit of this glaze overtop the mini meatloaves.

Bake for 40 minutes. The internal temperature of the meatloaves should be between 160°F and 165°F (71°C –74°C).

FREEZING Get the cooked meatloaves right into the freezer—bacteria flourish between 40°F and 140°F (4°C–60°C). Once the loaves have firmed up, put them into freezer bags. The faster you freeze food, the smaller the ice crystals will be, which means less damage to your lovingly prepared meals.

To reheat, either thaw the meatloaves in the refrigerator overnight and then warm them up in a 375°F (190°C) oven for 10 minutes, or bake them from frozen at 375°F (190°C) for 20 minutes.

Tilapia Tacos
with Fresh Lime

I STARTED MAKING THIS DISH when Scarlett was still quite wee. With no forks or knives required, she loved smashing the fish, and whatever else she felt inclined to grab, into a tattered tortilla. Today, she's far more particular about her plate (no food touching, please!) but the fun is still there—spooning on that yogurt mix is messy business! LK

Prep time: 10 minutes
Total time: 25 minutes
Makes: 4 servings

2 Tbsp (30 ml) + 2 tsp (10 ml) fresh
    lime juice
2 Tbsp (30 ml) extra virgin olive oil
½ tsp (2 ml) salt, divided
3 tilapia fillets
8 whole wheat flour tortillas
⅓ cup (80 ml) Greek yogurt
¼ cup (60 ml) chopped cilantro
2 Tbsp (30 ml) low-fat mayonnaise
½ head of lettuce, chopped

Preheat the oven to 425°F (220°C). Spray a rimmed baking sheet with cooking spray.

In a small bowl, whisk together 2 Tbsp (30 ml) lime juice with the oil and ¼ tsp (1 ml) of the salt for the marinade. Place the tilapia on the prepared baking sheet and spoon the marinade overtop.

Place the tilapia in the oven and bake for about 10 minutes. Give it the eagle eye so it doesn't overcook. When the fish flakes with a fork, get it out. Let cool for a few minutes. Transfer the tilapia to a large bowl and flake it apart using a fork. Set aside.

Reduce the oven temperature to 250°F (120°C).

Wrap the tortillas in a damp dish towel and place them in a medium-size casserole dish. Cover the dish with its lid or some aluminum foil. Warm the tortillas in the oven for about 10 minutes.

In a bowl, whisk together the yogurt, cilantro, mayonnaise, the 2 tsp (10 ml) lime juice and the remaining ¼ tsp (1 ml) salt.

Arrange the yogurt mix, chopped lettuce, warm tortillas and fish on the table and allow each family member to free-style their taco on the assembly line.

Shrimp with Bacon and Polenta

WHEN YOU THINK OF pantry-based meals, do tuna casseroles come to mind? Me too. Not that I don't love a good tuna casserole. When Ben comes home to find me whipping one up, he calls it the '50s. As in, "Oh, it's the '50s tonight, I love that!" Well, this is not the '50s. If you keep polenta in the cupboard and shrimp in the freezer (and you should, on both counts), you can arrive home at the end of the day with no plan for dinner and still have something amazing on the table in less than half an hour. CM

Prep time: 15 minutes
Total time: 25 minutes
Makes: 4 servings

5 cups (1.25 L) water
1 cup (250 ml) instant polenta
2 Tbsp (30 ml) olive oil
6 slices of bacon, chopped into bite-size pieces
2 cloves garlic, minced
1 can (28 oz/796 ml) whole tomatoes
1 lb (450 g) fresh or thawed frozen shrimp,
    peeled, deveined and washed
Small handful of parsley

Bring the water to a boil and slowly pour in the polenta. Bring the heat right down. Keep stirring and cook the polenta for 3 to 5 minutes. Remove from the heat and cover the pot.

Heat the olive oil in a large frying pan over medium heat, then add the bacon. Cook for a few minutes until the bacon is brown but not crispy. Add the garlic and cook for another minute or so. Add the tomatoes and break them up with a potato masher (gently, gently!). Allow the sauce to simmer for 15 minutes, or until it begins to thicken.

While the sauce is bubbling away, get your shrimp ready. Peel off the shells and tails (we left them on for this pic, as it makes them look more shrimpy, but I'd never serve them that way). If they're not already deveined, take a small, sharp knife and run it down the back of the shrimp. You're just making a very shallow cut. Use the tip of your knife to pull out the vein. Rinse all the shrimp under cold water to be sure they're clean. Drain them well.

Put the shrimp into the simmering sauce and stir. They'll cook quickly, about 3 minutes.

Give your polenta another stir. You may need to add a splash of warm water to loosen it up. Create a nest of polenta on a plate and then ladle the saucy shrimp onto it. Sprinkle parsley on top.

Crunchy Baked Fish and Chips

Here's our healthy take on a fast food favorite. All the crunch but much less fat than traditional battered fish and chips. We've even come up with a lighter version of tartar sauce! CM

Prep time: 10 minutes
Total time: 50 minutes
Makes: 4 servings

Fish and Chips

4 medium Yukon Gold potatoes,
    scrubbed and cut into wedges
2 Tbsp (30 ml) vegetable oil
4 small fillets of cod or halibut
1 egg
1 Tbsp (15 ml) milk
1 cup (250 ml) panko breadcrumbs
    (or traditional dried breadcrumbs)
2 Tbsp (30 ml) finely chopped fresh
    parsley or dill (use about half if
    you're using dried herbs)

Tartar Sauce

½ cup (125 ml) Greek yogurt
3 Tbsp (45 ml) fresh lemon juice
2 Tbsp (30 ml) finely diced cornichons
1 Tbsp (15 ml) chopped fresh dill
1 tsp (5 ml) Dijon mustard

Preheat the oven to 450°F (230°C). Place a baking sheet in the oven.

In a large bowl, toss your potato wedges in the vegetable oil until they're lightly but completely coated. Use an oven mitt to take your hot baking sheet out of the oven and spread the potatoes out evenly across it. Pop it back in the oven. Bake the wedges for 20 minutes, then use a spatula or fork to turn them over. Bake for another 10 minutes.

Rinse the fish under cold, running water and pat dry. Get your work station ready!

Whisk the egg with the milk and place it in a shallow bowl. Toss the panko with the parsley or dill and spread it out on a plate. Have a clean plate at the ready. Dip each piece of fish into the egg mixture and then dredge it in the panko. You may have to press the panko into the fish a bit. Put the fish on the clean plate while you dredge the rest.

Take your baking sheet out of the oven and push the potatoes out to the edges. Place the fish in the middle and put it all back in the oven for 10 minutes. Break into the middle of a piece of fish to check for doneness.

While the fish is cooking, make the tartar sauce. Stir together the yogurt, lemon juice, cornichons, dill and mustard in a small bowl and serve a dollop with each plate of fish and chips.

Salmon Dinner Salad

W<small>E LIKE TO CALL THIS</small> made-for-picky-kids meal a DIY Dinner. With all the different ingredients, it's easy to make up as many dinner plates as you have diners. Julian can skip the lettuce, Esme can eat around the dressing and so on. This is one of our summertime favorites. It's easy to chip away at its preparation during the day so all you have left to do by dinnertime is broil the salmon and the corn. CM

Prep time: 20 minutes
Total time: 45 minutes
Makes: 4 servings

1 cup (250 ml) frozen corn
8 small red potatoes, cut in half
1 head tender lettuce (Boston or butter)
2 ¾-lb (375 g) salmon fillets
1 Tbsp (15 ml) olive oil
⅓ cup (80 ml) fresh lemon juice
Salt and pepper
1 avocado
6–7 plum tomatoes
½ cup (125 ml) plain yogurt
¼ cup (60 ml) finely chopped fresh dill
1 Tbsp (15 ml) honey

Pour the frozen corn into a small bowl so it can thaw as you work. Boil the potatoes until tender. Drain and set aside. Wash, dry and slice lettuce into ribbons. Turn the broiler on (to low if your broiler has a high/low setting).

Rinse your fish with cold, running water and pat dry with paper towel. Place the fillets on a rimmed baking sheet skin side down. Brush with the olive oil and 1 Tbsp (15 ml) of the lemon juice and sprinkle with a pinch of salt and pepper. Shake the thawed corn all around the salmon. Place under the broiler and cook for 5 to 10 minutes. Keep an eye on it! The salmon will become opaque and the corn will begin to char. Pull out your baking sheet and use a fork to break into the salmon and check that it's cooked through. Set aside and allow to cool a bit.

Use a sharp knife to cut the avocado in half and remove the pit. Score the flesh of the avocado into squares with a regular table knife and then gently run the knife under the flesh to flick out the squares. Slice the tomatoes lengthwise.

Get out a nice, big platter. Cover it with a bed of sliced lettuce. Arrange the potatoes, avocado and tomatoes evenly across the lettuce. Once the salmon is cool enough to handle, gently peel off the skin. Break the fish into bite-size pieces with your hands and arrange them over the salad. Sprinkle the corn overtop everything.

To make the dressing, place the remaining lemon juice in a jar with the yogurt, dill, honey and a pinch of salt and pepper. Put a lid on the jar and shake well. Either dress the salad or place the dressing on the table so your family can help themselves.

Salmon Cakes

'M LUCKY TO HAVE TWO fish-loving kids. I don't need to find ways to sneak fish into our meals, but if I did I'd have another reason to love these salmon cakes. They're easy and delicious. The recipe calls for tinned salmon so you don't have to figure out where you're going to find fresh fish when you decide you want them! CM

Prep time: 1 hour 20 minutes
Total time: 1 hour 40 minutes
Makes: 10–12 cakes

2 large Yukon Gold potatoes, peeled and
    chopped into 2-inch (5 cm) dice
1 leek
2 cans (each 7 oz/200 g) salmon
¼ cup (60 ml) mayonnaise
2 Tbsp (30 ml) finely chopped fresh dill
Salt and pepper
¼ cup (60 ml) all-purpose flour
2 eggs
1 ½ cups (375 ml) sesame seeds
2 Tbsp (30 ml) vegetable oil
Plain yogurt for garnish
Fresh dill for garnish

Boil a large pot of salted water to a boil and add the potatoes. Simmer until tender, about 10 minutes. Drain and mash well. You'll end up with about 2 cups (500 ml) of mashed potatoes.

Trim the root end and most of the green part of your leek. Slice it lengthwise and rinse halves thoroughly (a lot of dirt hides in there, so take your time with this!). Then slice as thinly as you can.

Open and drain the salmon. In a large bowl, gently mix the salmon with the mashed potatoes, leek, mayonnaise, dill and salt and pepper to taste. You want this mixture to be well combined but still chunky.

Form the mixture into 12 patties, about 2 ½ inches (6 cm) across and ½ inch (1 cm) thick. Place the patties on a plate (or two), cover with plastic wrap and refrigerate for at least 1 hour, but you could leave them overnight.

Spread the flour out on a plate. Whisk the eggs in a shallow dish and spread the sesame seeds out on another plate. Dredge the patties in the flour, then dip them in the egg, then press them into the seeds. Place the patties on a clean platter.

Heat a bit of vegetable oil in a frying pan over medium-high heat. Gently place the patties in the pan—don't crowd that pan or you'll have a job flipping them—and cook them for about 5 minutes on each side. Serve with a dollop of plain yogurt and a pinch of fresh dill.

Don't Call Them Picky, for Heaven's Sake

I ONLY HAVE ONE CHILD, but I was blessed with an eater. If you have a multi-kid family, someone, somewhere along the way, is going to be a non-eater. It's just the way of the universe. Even though my kid happily tore through her broccoli as a toddler (and still does), I have witnessed my friends struggle with some seriously discerning eaters. One friend used to stuff egg yolks into the center of Cheerios in an effort to get extra nutrients into her persnickety child. (It didn't work. She'd spit them out.) If you're confronted with one of these children, don't despair. We have some strategies for you. And remember, like most challenges with children, this too shall pass. Or you can just sell the kid.

- Try to remember that pickiness is almost always a stage. It's best not to label children "picky" or to discuss their eating habits in front of them. You don't want to give them permission to settle into the role.

- Try to model a healthy and adventurous approach to eating. Kids aren't going to want to eat anything you don't.

- Get the picky eater in an apron and on duty. Children are more likely to try a dish they've helped prepare. And it doesn't hurt to make a big fuss about Sofia's scrumptious spinach to everyone at the table.

- As a former picky eater, I can tell you it was less daunting to tackle a plate full of foreign foods if I recognized some familiar friends there too. In other words, if you're going to ask your child to eat something you know will be an issue, try pairing it with something he loves to eat.

- Finally, picky eating is all about control. As hard as it is, when your kid tells you that the broccoli she ate yesterday is now gross/disgusting/icky/yucky, just shrug it off. If there's less conflict associated with mealtime, your child will be more likely to let down her guard and try something new. LK

Grilled Shrimp Salad

I'S ONLY IN THE LAST COUPLE OF YEARS that I've become comfortable with the barbecue. It's embarrassing to admit, but I used to leave grilling to Ben. But his work schedule can be so nuts in the summer that I needed to get over myself. However, I may have reclaimed the grill from the man of the house but my approach is still pretty girly—I use it to make salads! This one incorporates some of my favorite flavors: lime, cumin and garlic. The black beans make it substantial enough that even guys feel like they're getting a real meal. CM

Prep time: 1 hour 20 minutes
Total time: 1 hour 30 minutes
Makes: 4 servings

Marinade and Shrimp

1 lb (450 g) large shrimp (frozen is fine,
    just let them thaw before starting)
2 cloves garlic, minced
1 Tbsp (15 ml) vegetable oil
1 Tbsp (15 ml) fresh lime juice
1 tsp (5 ml) soy sauce
1 tsp (5 ml) sesame oil
Pepper
4–5 wooden skewers

Salad

2–3 cobs of corn, shucked
1 can (19 oz/540 ml) black beans,
    drained and rinsed
1 red, yellow or orange bell pepper, diced
½ cup (125 ml) chopped cilantro
1 avocado, diced
1 head Boston lettuce, chopped

Dressing

¼ cup (60 ml) vegetable oil
3 Tbsp (45 ml) fresh lime juice
½ tsp (2 ml) ground cumin
½ tsp (2 ml) salt
¼ tsp (1 ml) pepper

See overleaf for preparation

Peel and devein the shrimp. To devein them, run a small, sharp knife down the back of the shrimp—you only need to make a very shallow cut, and you'll be able to pull out the vein. Rinse the shrimp in cold, running water to be sure they're clean.

For the marinade, mix together the garlic, vegetable oil, lime juice, soy sauce, sesame oil and pepper to taste in a shallow bowl. Add the shrimp and toss to make sure they all get thoroughly coated with the marinade. Cover the bowl and place in the refrigerator for at least 1 hour.

Place the wooden skewers in a shallow bowl of water and let them soak for at least 30 minutes before they go onto the grill.

Lightly oil and heat up your grill.

For the salad, place the shucked corn on the grill for 15 minutes, rotating the corn every 5 minutes. The cobs will just begin to char. Remove them from the heat and let them cool for a few minutes before running a knife down the cobs to slice off the kernels.

Place the beans, diced bell pepper and cilantro in a bowl with the corn and stir to combine. Gently fold in the avocado, you don't want it to get mushy.

For the dressing, whisk together the oil, lime juice, cumin, salt and pepper in a small bowl and pour about half of it over the bean mixture. Stir and give it a taste. You may want to add a bit more dressing.

Take the shrimp out of the refrigerator. Put about three shrimp onto each skewer. Go through the tail and the top so that they can lie flat on the grill. Cook them on the barbecue for about 3 minutes each side. They'll become a bright pink. Use tongs to remove them from the grill. Allow them to cool slightly before sliding them off the skewers.

On a serving plate, arrange the chopped lettuce and then pile the bean mixture on top. Now place the shrimp all over the salad. You might want to finish with a final drizzle of salad dressing.

Table Talk

I DON'T WANT TO TALK ABOUT food at the table.
Okay, tell me my lemon linguini is fantastic, but then let's
move on, shall we? Nothing breaks my dinnertime spirit
like an exchange over how many bites need to be consumed
before dessert will be allowed. Please. Manners matter, and
I want my kids to eat with their mouths closed, to be sure,
but I also want to teach them about another level of nicety—
conversation. To set a good example, I try to come to the table
with an anecdote for them. The more extreme the better.
They love it when I tell them about a phone call that made
me so mad I could have spit or some epic blunder that nearly
wiped out my computer. But not all dinner theater has to be
the retelling of our days. Ben's been working with Esme on
how to tell jokes. Well, a joke, because they've been practicing
the same one forever. It's a long, involved joke that ends with
a play on words. She can almost get through the whole thing
now without prompts. She told it the other night when we
had friends over for dinner. Of course, our lovely pals slapped
their knees with laughter, and Esme beamed with pride.
Soon she won't need any prompting to tell a joke or share
an anecdote of her own. But for now, "A piece of string
walked into a bar . . ." CM

Tuna Steaks over Soba Noodles

'M A BIG FAN OF MEALS like this one that allow expensive ingredients, in this case tuna steaks, to go a little further than they might normally. I really love the light, bright flavors of this dish, and my kids love that the vegetables are crunchy and almost raw! CM

Prep time: 35 minutes
Total time: 45 minutes
Makes: 4 servings

Tuna

¼ cup (60 ml) low-sodium soy sauce

¼ cup (60 ml) rice wine vinegar

1 Tbsp (15 ml) sesame oil

1 clove garlic, minced

2 ¾-lb (375 g) tuna steaks

1 package (8 oz/225 g) soba noodles

¼ cup (60 ml) sesame seeds

1 Tbsp (15 ml) vegetable oil

½ cup (125 ml) matchsticked carrots

½ cup (125 ml) matchsticked peeled cucumber

½ cup (125 ml) matchsticked red bell pepper

½ cup (125 ml) bok choy
(the white cut into matchsticks, the greens sliced into ribbons)

2 scallions, the green and just a bit of the white sliced thinly

Dressing

¼ cup (60 ml) vegetable oil

2 Tbsp (30 ml) sesame oil

2 Tbsp (30 ml) fresh lemon juice

2 Tbsp (30 ml) rice wine vinegar

Salt and pepper

Whisk together the soy sauce, rice wine vinegar, sesame oil and minced garlic to make a marinade. Pour it into a shallow pan. Rinse the tuna steaks under cold water, pat dry and place them in the marinade, turning once or twice to coat. Cover the pan with plastic wrap and refrigerate for 30 minutes.

Bring a large pot of water to boil.

In a small bowl, mix together the dressing ingredients.

Spread the sesame seeds out on a clean plate. Take the fish out of the marinade and press the steaks into the seeds. Turn them over and press the seeds onto the other side.

Add soba noodles to the boiling water and cook according to the package instructions.

Heat a large frying pan over medium-high heat and add the 1 Tbsp (15 ml) of vegetable oil. Place the fish in the pan. Depending on how thick your steaks are, cook for about 3 minutes on each side.

Drain the soba noodles and pour them out onto a large serving platter. Toss in the matchsticked vegetables and the dressing. Take the tuna steaks off the heat and slice them against the grain into 1-inch (2.5 cm) strips. Lay the fish over the noodles, sprinkle the scallions overtop and serve.

Rosemary Dijon Rack of Lamb

D AN AND SCARLETT ARE BIG FANS of this dish. I'm a devotee of it because it doesn't require a lot of shopping, cutting, marinating and cooking. And while you don't always think of lamb for a Tuesday night, its ease does lend itself to being on the menu. **LK**

Prep time: 15 minutes
Total time: 60 minutes
Makes: 4 servings

2 racks lamb (about 3 lb/1.5 kg)
    with fat already trimmed off
Salt and pepper
1 Tbsp (15 ml) grapeseed oil
2 cloves garlic, minced
3 Tbsp (45 ml) Dijon mustard
1 Tbsp (15 ml) fresh rosemary, plus a few
    sprigs for garnish
1 Tbsp (15 ml) olive oil
1 Tbsp (15 ml) fresh lemon juice

Preheat the oven to 450°F (230°C) and place the oven rack in the center of the oven.

Season the lamb with salt and pepper.

In a heavy frying pan, heat the grapeseed oil over high heat. Add the lamb and sear the flesh on each side until golden brown, about 1 to 2 minutes. Remove from the pan and set aside to rest for a few minutes.

Meanwhile, whisk together the garlic, Dijon mustard, rosemary, olive oil and lemon juice. Place the lamb in a shallow dish and brush the marinade over the meaty part. Then, with the rib ends up, press the racks of lamb together to interlink the bones. Separate their bases by about 1 inch (2.5 cm) to stabilize them. Place on a greased cooking rack in a roasting pan, and drizzle over any remaining marinade.

Cover the exposed ribs with aluminum foil to prevent charring. Roast for 10 minutes. Reduce the temperature to 325°F (160°C) and roast for another 30 to 40 minutes, or until a meat thermometer registers 145°F (63°C) for medium-rare.

Transfer to a warm platter, tent with aluminum foil and let stand for 10 minutes. Remove all the foil and carve between the bones. Garnish with fresh sprigs of rosemary.

Ginger Pork over Pasta

THIS DISH HAS A RICH HISTORY. Passed from a mother to a son then through friends, it arrived in my kitchen as a far more kid-friendly dish thanks to tweaks made by my neighbor Anne. No longer featuring peanut oil and serious amounts of chilies, as it did in its earlier incarnations, the recipe still has a snap of flavor courtesy of the fresh ginger and garlic. Make it your own by switching up the vegetables or trying it over rice. LK

Prep time: 10 minutes
Total time: 35 minutes
Makes: 4 servings

8 oz (225 g) rigatoni pasta
2 Tbsp (30 ml) grapeseed oil
1 onion, chopped
½ cup (125 ml) chopped mushrooms
1 lb (450 g) minced pork
8 cloves garlic, minced
2 Tbsp (30 ml) freshly grated ginger
Salt and pepper
2 ½ cups (625 ml) chicken stock, plus
    more as needed
1 cup (250 ml) sugar snap peas
2 Tbsp (30 ml) chopped green onion
1 Tbsp (15 ml) chopped cilantro

Cook the pasta according to the package instructions. Drain and set aside.

Heat the grapeseed oil in a wok or deep frying pan over medium heat. Add the onion and sauté until softened. Mix in the mushrooms and sauté for about 2 minutes until they start to soften.

Stir in the minced pork. Sauté the pork for about 5 minutes until it is cooked and then add the garlic and ginger, and salt and pepper to taste. Mix until well combined and simmer for a few minutes. Add the stock and sugar snap peas. There should be enough stock covering the meat and vegetables to make it a bit soupy. Sprinkle in the chopped green onion and stir until combined.

Ladle the pork mixture over a serving of pasta and garnish with cilantro. Serve immediately.

Spaghetti and Meatballs

THIS ICONIC FAMILY MEAL is perfect for those Sundays when you have a bit of time in the late afternoon to get things started, the kids are magically occupied and getting along, your favorite songs are coming up on shuffle and all is right with the world. What? That doesn't happen much in your house? Mine neither, to be honest. But everyone is happy to come to the table for this dinner, eat with abandon and thank the cook. Sometimes that's all it takes to make your world feel right. CM

Prep time: 20 minutes
Total time: 1 hour
Makes: 6 servings

2 Tbsp (30 ml) olive oil
1 onion, chopped quite fine
2–3 cloves garlic, minced
¼ tsp (1 ml) ground nutmeg
¼ tsp (1 ml) ground cinnamon
¼ tsp (1 ml) chili flakes
1 tsp (5 ml) salt
½ tsp (2 ml) pepper
1 can (28 oz/796 ml) whole tomatoes
2 Tbsp (30 ml) red wine vinegar
1 lb (450 g) ground beef
½ cup (125 ml) panko breadcrumbs
    or traditional dried breadcrumbs
½ cup (125 ml) grated Parmesan cheese,
    plus extra to serve at the table
1 egg, whisked
Zest of ½ lemon, minced
1 lb (450 g) whole wheat spaghetti

In a large pot, warm up 1 Tbsp (15 ml) of the olive oil over medium heat. Sauté the onion and garlic until they begin to soften, 3 to 5 minutes. Add the nutmeg, cinnamon, chili flakes, salt and pepper. Cook for another couple of minutes until it smells amazing and everything is soft.

Remove half the onion mixture from the pot and place it in a large bowl to cool.

Add the tomatoes and red wine vinegar to the remaining onion mixture in the pot. Break up the tomatoes with the back of a wooden spoon or a potato masher. Reduce the heat and allow the sauce to simmer away as you make your meatballs.

To the onion mixture in the bowl, add the beef, panko or traditional breadcrumbs, ½ cup (125 ml) Parmesan, egg and lemon zest. You could use a fork to combine it but the best tools really are your hands. Take off your rings! Form the meat mixture into small meatballs, about 1 ½ inches (4 cm) across. Try to keep them fairly uniform so they'll cook at the same rate.

Put a big pot of water on to boil for the pasta. Add a big pinch of salt to the water.

In a large frying pan, warm up the remaining 1 Tbsp (15 ml) of olive oil over medium-high heat. Working in batches, brown the meatballs. Don't crowd them or the pan won't stay hot enough. Keep nudging them around every few minutes so that they cook evenly all over. It will take about 10 minutes for the meatballs to cook all the way through but you can break into one to be sure. Once the meatballs are cooked, add them to the sauce and give it all a gentle stir.

Put your spaghetti into water that is roiling (really, really boiling!). As the noodles begin to sag, give them a stir so they submerge. Give the pasta one last good stir so the noodles don't stick to each other. Cook according to package instructions. Just before the pasta is finished, scoop out ½ cup (125 ml) of cooking water. Then drain the pasta. Give your sauce another stir, and if it's too thick, add a splash of your pasta water. The water will loosen up the sauce, and the starch in it will give it a gloss and a structure.

Use tongs to twirl a small heap of noodles on each plate. Ladle on some sauce and sprinkle on some more grated Parmesan.

WHAT'S SO GREAT ABOUT TOMATOES? The lycopene in tomatoes not only gives them their bright hue but may also help guard against some cancers, including breast and prostate. An antioxidant powerhouse, this vine fruit can also be counted on for a healthy dose of vitamins A, C and K. LK

Beef Lettuce Wraps

WE DON'T EAT a whole lot of red meat but sometimes nothing but a steak will do. If we're going to have beef, though, I prefer meals like this, where it's just one element among many, not the king of the plate. CM

Prep time: 1 hour
Total time: 1 hour 20 minutes
Makes: 4 servings

Marinade

2 cloves garlic, minced

1 tsp (5 ml) minced fresh ginger

¼ cup (60 ml) low-sodium soy sauce

2 Tbsp (30 ml) fresh lime juice

1 Tbsp (15 ml) sesame oil

1 Tbsp (15 ml) fish sauce

1 tsp (5 ml) Sriracha

Steak

1 lb (450 g) flank steak

1 cup (250 ml) whole grain jasmine rice

1 head soft lettuce, such as Boston or Bibb

½ cup (125 ml) finely chopped cucumber

½ cup (125 ml) matchsticked carrot

½ cup (125 ml) matchsticked red bell pepper

Handful of chopped cilantro

Dipping Sauce

2 cloves garlic, minced

1 green onion, chopped

2 Tbsp (30 ml) low-sodium soy sauce

1 Tbsp (15 ml) rice wine vinegar

1 Tbsp (15 ml) water

1 tsp (5 ml) Sriracha

1 tsp (5 ml) sesame oil

½ tsp (2 ml) sugar

For the marinade, mix the garlic and ginger with the soy sauce, lime juice, sesame oil, fish sauce and Sriracha in a baking dish.

Place the steak in the marinade and turn it over once or twice to thoroughly coat. Cover the whole thing with plastic wrap and get in the refrigerator for at least 1 hour—but overnight would be even better.

Cook the rice according to the package instructions.

Pull apart and wash a head of lettuce. Dry the leaves with a spinner and stack the leaves on a plate. Arrange all the extras—the cucumber, carrots, pepper and cilantro—in small serving dishes.

Prepare the dipping sauce by mixing together the garlic, green onion, soy sauce, rice wine vinegar, water, Sriracha, sesame oil and sugar.

Place the rice in a serving bowl or dish and arrange it along with all the extras on the table. You can cook the steak on the barbecue or under the broiler for about 3 minutes a side. Allow the meat to rest, covered, for 10 minutes before slicing it into thin strips, across the grain. Lay the meat out on a platter.

To assemble, hold a lettuce leaf in one hand and build your choice of ingredients on top of the other. Yes, it's going to be messy! Encourage everyone to make up their own combinations.

Nana Molly's Stuffed Artichokes

M Y GRANDMOTHER WAS ONE of those legendary family chefs. Food was second nature to her, and if you asked her what was in something she'd slyly tell you "love." I have so many memories of her in the kitchen, apron on and her mouth full of the food she was crafting, giggling with my mom. When I asked my mom to pinpoint Nana's best dish, she couldn't choose just one but said she missed her stuffed artichokes the most. Nana served them as a side dish, but I think they make a great appetizer. These artichokes look like my grandmother's and they taste great too, but they're not quite the same. Maybe Nana's love really was the secret to her food. **LK**

Prep time: 20 minutes
Total time: 1 hour
Makes: 4–6 servings

6 fresh artichokes, cleaned
1 cup (250 ml) fresh Italian breadcrumbs
5–6 cloves garlic, minced
¼ cup (60 ml) grated Parmesan cheese
¼ cup (60 ml) chopped fresh parsley
½ tsp (2 ml) chopped fresh oregano
¼ cup (60 ml) extra virgin olive oil
Salt and pepper

Preheat the oven to 350°F (180°C).

Cut off the artichoke stems. Clip ½ inch (1 cm) off the top of each artichoke and then clip whatever other leaf tips remain. Gently spread the leaves apart (but you don't want to snap them) using your thumb and index finger.

In a large bowl, mix the breadcrumbs, garlic, Parmesan cheese, parsley and oregano with a few drops of the olive oil to help bind it all together.

Press a teaspoonful (5 ml) of bread mixture into each artichoke leaf, beginning from the outside edge and working toward the center.

Sit the artichokes in two large baking dishes. Fill the dishes with water about halfway, just short of the first row of leaves. Cover the dishes with aluminum foil and place them in the oven, bringing the liquid to a slow simmer for 30 to 40 minutes, or until the leaves are tender.

Remove the artichokes from the oven and use tongs to place them on a serving dish. Drizzle the tops with the remaining olive oil and serve.

Pears with Goat Cheese and Cranberries

EVEN WITHOUT SOUP TUREENS and gold leaf place cards, entertaining can still be elegant. (Okay, I never use gold leaf place cards.) That's why we love this appetizer. Not the least bit fussy, it can happen in a snap. I've even been known to let Scarlett put it together while I, well, put myself together. **LK**

Prep time: 10 minutes

Total time: 10 minutes

Makes: 8–10 servings

2 green Anjou pears, cored and sliced

1 Tbsp (15 ml) orange or fresh lemon juice

½ cup (125 ml) softened goat cheese

2 Tbsp (30 ml) pistachio pieces

2 Tbsp (30 ml) dried cranberries

1 tsp (5 ml) honey

Core pears and cut into about 12 slices. Toss them in the orange or lemon juice to keep from browning.

In a small bowl, mix together the cheese, pistachio pieces, cranberries and honey.

Spread the cheese mixture on the widest part of each pear slice. Arrange the pear slices on a serving tray and serve. If you're not serving immediately, cover with plastic wrap and refrigerate until needed.

Glazed Green Vegetables

Roasted Vegetables

Butternut Squash and Apple Purée

Beet Slaw

Super Sides

I'T'S EASY TO LOSE MEAL-PLANNING momentum once you've decided on a main. I get it. I mean you were brilliant enough to take the chicken thighs out of the freezer in the morning. Isn't that enough? Sadly, no. We've put together a collection of our favorite approaches to vegetable dishes. I say approaches because you should feel free to try different ingredients than the ones we're showing here. Add apples to your roasted veggies, try glazing sliced summer squash, throw fennel into your next slaw, purée a sweet potato . . . you get the idea. CM

See overleaf for recipes

Glazed Green Vegetables

JUST A LITTLE BIT more special than plain old steamed veggies, these have a light yet sweet glaze that makes them appealing to even the most hard-hearted vegetablephobe. CM

Prep time: 5 minutes

Total time: 15 minutes

Makes: 4 servings

1 bunch asparagus, trimmed
2 handfuls green beans, trimmed
3 Tbsp (45 ml) butter
2 Tbsp (30 ml) sugar
Salt and pepper
1 cup (250 ml) peas (frozen are fine)

Place the asparagus and beans in a medium-size frying pan. Add enough water to not quite half cover the vegetables. Add the butter, sugar and a pinch of salt and pepper. Place a lid on top.

Simmer over medium heat until the vegetables are almost tender, 3 minutes.

Add the peas and cook for another minute. Shake the frying pan so everything gets covered in the glaze. Check the beans to see if they're as tender as you like and serve.

Roasted Vegetables

There's nothing more satisfying than the warm, caramelized sweetness of veggies roasted in the oven, and this dish definitely delivers. **LK**

Prep time: 15 minutes
Total time: 55 minutes
Makes: 4 servings

5 white potatoes, cut into quarters
4 medium carrots, peeled and cut into pieces
2 sweet potatoes, peeled and cut into small cubes
2 beets, peeled and cut into quarters
1 onion, cut into quarters
½ cup (125 ml) extra virgin olive oil
1 Tbsp (15 ml) salt
2–3 bay leaves
A few sprigs of sage
1 bulb of garlic, stem trimmed

Preheat the oven to 400°F (200°C).

In a large bowl, mix together the potatoes, carrots, sweet potatoes, beets and onion. In a small bowl, whisk the oil with the salt. Pour over the vegetables and toss to evenly and thoroughly coat them. Add the bay leaves and sage and toss again. Spread the veggies evenly on a large roasting pan.

Roast in the oven for 20 minutes. Remove pan and add garlic bulb. Return pan to oven for another 20-25 minutes, stirring every 10 minutes, until the vegetables are brown on the outside and tender inside.

Butternut Squash and Apple Purée

WHY STOP MAKING PURÉES once your babies aren't babies? This sweet and savory combo is one of our favorites. CM

Prep time: 15 minutes
Total time: 25 minutes
Makes: 4 servings

1 lb (450 g) butternut squash, peeled,
    cored and cut into 2-inch (5 cm) cubes,
    about 3 cups (750 ml)
3 fresh sage leaves
1 cup (250 ml) peeled, cored and chopped apple
    (preferably something sweet, like
    Honey Crisp or Gala)
1 Tbsp (15 ml) butter
½ tsp (2 ml) ground nutmeg
Salt and pepper

Bring a large pot of water to boil. Add the squash and the sage leaves. Simmer for 5 minutes. Add the apple and cook for another 3 minutes. Reserve 1 cup (250 ml) of the cooking water before draining.

Put the squash and apple in a blender, or return them to the pot and use an immersion blender to blend until smooth. Stir in the butter, nutmeg and a pinch of salt and pepper. You may need to add some of the reserved cooking water now if the purée is too thick.

Beet Slaw

'VE ALWAYS BEEN a big fan of beets, but I used to wait for other people to cook them. Once I got over the hump of having to scrub down like a surgeon after cooking with them, I found that I loved using this sweet and heart-healthy root vegetable in a variety of dishes, like this oh-so-simple side. LK

Prep time: 30 minutes
Total time: 30 minutes
Makes: 4 servings

Slaw

3 medium beets
4 large carrots, peeled
1 English cucumber
¼ cup (60 ml) cashews, roughly chopped
1 Tbsp (15 ml) chopped cilantro

Dressing

½ cup (125 ml) buttermilk (you do want the
    creaminess of real buttermilk for this one.)
1 Tbsp (15 ml) apple cider vinegar
1 Tbsp (15 ml) maple syrup
1 Tbsp (15 ml) poppy seeds
Salt and pepper

For the slaw, parboil the beets in a medium-size saucepan full of boiling water for about 10 minutes. You want the beets to still have a little bite to them. Drain the beets and run them under cold water to remove the skin. Set aside to cool. Using a mandoline, carefully grate the carrots and cucumber into matchsticks. Repeat with the cooled beets.

For the dressing, whisk together the buttermilk, vinegar and maple syrup with the poppy seeds. Add salt and pepper to taste.

On a medium-size platter, lightly mix together the vegetables and drizzle with half the dressing. Garnish with cashews and cilantro. Serve immediately with the remaining dressing on the side.

WHAT'S SO GREAT ABOUT BEETS? The deep purple-red insides of a beet aren't just beautiful, they're rich in nutrition. Dense with vitamins and minerals, beets also contain powerful phytonutrients called betalains, which act as bouncers for your body's toxins. To get the most out of these sweet (but tough!) veggies, try not to overcook them. CM

Great Grains

WE LOVE POTATOES as much as anyone (which is to say a lot), but we can't let them hog space on our dinner plates every night. Branching out into the world of grains makes for much more interesting meals, not to mention the nutritional boost grains bring to the table. We're sharing recipes that use our families' favorite grains, but of course there are many more to try, such as barley, quinoa and kamut. CM

Couscous Pilaf

Farro and Roasted Vegetables

Lentil Salad

Currant Apricot Rice

See overleaf for recipes

Couscous Pilaf

THIS SIDE DISH IS FULL of flavor and texture with soft cheese and crunchy vegetables. It's the perfect dish to bring along to a potluck dinner or barbecue. CM

Prep time: 5 minutes
Total time: 25 minutes
Makes: 6 servings

Couscous

1 Tbsp (15 ml) olive oil
1 onion, finely chopped
1 cup (250 ml) whole grain Israeli couscous
1 cup (250 ml) low-sodium chicken
    or vegetable stock
¼ cup (60 ml) water
½ cup (125 ml) finely chopped cucumber
½ cup (125 ml) finely chopped yellow bell pepper
½ cup (125 ml) finely chopped tomato
¼ cup (60 ml) crumbled feta cheese
Small handful of fresh mint, chopped
Small handful of fresh parsley, chopped

Dressing

¼ cup (60 ml) olive oil
2 Tbsp (30 ml) red wine vinegar
1 tsp (5 ml) Dijon mustard
1 tsp (5 ml) honey
Salt and pepper

For the couscous, warm the olive oil in a large saucepan over medium heat. Add the onion and allow to soften and just start to brown. Now add the couscous and stir so that the pearls become covered in oil. Let the couscous sauté for 3 to 5 minutes, stirring occasionally. Pour in the stock and water and give everything a good stir. Allow the liquid to come to a boil, then reduce the heat and simmer for 15 to 20 minutes. You want the couscous to be al dente, not mushy. Remove from the heat.

In a serving bowl, mix the cucumber, bell pepper, tomato, feta, mint and parsley with the cooked couscous.

For the dressing, mix together the olive oil, vinegar, mustard, honey and salt and pepper to taste. Add it to the couscous and mix to combine. You can serve this dish right away or cover it and put it in the refrigerator for a bit for even better flavors.

Farro and Roasted Vegetables

F YOU'VE NEVER TRIED FARRO BEFORE you're in for a treat. It's a great alternative to rice or potatoes, and reminds me of barley. We love this dish in the fall and winter with its mellow, earthy flavors. CM

Prep time: 10 minutes
Total time: 1 hour
Makes: 6 servings

Farro and Roasted Vegetables
5 cups (1.25 L) water
1 cup (250 ml) farro
1 tsp (5 ml) salt
1 cup (250 ml) diced portobello mushrooms
1 cup (250 ml) diced zucchini
1 cup (250 ml) diced red or yellow bell pepper
2 Tbsp (30 ml) olive oil
2 Tbsp (30 ml) balsamic vinegar
1 Tbsp (15 ml) fresh thyme
¼ cup (60 ml) roughly chopped hazelnuts
¼ cup (60 ml) goat cheese

Dressing
1 Tbsp (15 ml) olive oil
1 Tbsp (15 ml) fresh lemon juice
Salt and pepper

Preheat the oven to 450°F (230°C).

Put the water in a large saucepan and add the farro and salt. Bring the water to the boil and then reduce the heat a bit so it simmers away for 45 to 50 minutes until the farro is tender but chewy.

In a roasting pan, toss the mushrooms, zucchini and bell pepper with the oil, vinegar and thyme. Bake in the hot oven for about 30 minutes, until everything is very soft.

Toast the hazelnuts in a hot, dry frying pan on the stovetop for 2 or 3 minutes until they smell great and just start to darken.

Drain the farro. Remove the roasting pan from the oven. Tip the farro into the vegetables and stir everything around to combine the flavors.

Transfer to the serving bowl you're going to use. Toss in the cheese and hazelnuts and stir gently.

For the dressing, whisk the oil with the lemon juice and salt and pepper, and drizzle over the farro and veggies.

Lentil Salad

W E LOVE LENTILS! (When was the last time you read that?) Not only are they quick and easy to prepare, the little legume absorbs the flavors of everything you cook with it. And don't let their small size fool you—they deliver large on nutrients like fiber and iron. LK

Prep time: 10 minutes

Total time: 30 minutes

Makes: 4–6 servings

1 ½ cups (375 ml) dried brown lentils, rinsed and picked over

1 bay leaf

3 Tbsp (45 ml) grapeseed oil

6 baby spinach leaves, cut small

1 medium onion, diced

4 cloves garlic, minced

1 stalk celery, diced

1 large carrot, diced

1 tsp (5 ml) chopped fresh parsley

1 Tbsp (15 ml) red wine vinegar

Salt and pepper

½ cup (125 ml) grated Parmesan cheese

In a saucepan over medium heat, cover the lentils and bay leaf with water about 1 inch (2.5 cm) over the top of the lentils. Simmer for about 15 minutes or until the lentils are soft but not falling apart.

Meanwhile, in a medium-size frying pan, heat the grapeseed oil over medium heat and sauté the spinach, onion, garlic, celery, carrot and parsley for about 5 minutes, until the vegetables are soft but still crisp. Set aside.

Drain the lentils and remove and discard the bay leaf. In a medium-size bowl, mix the lentils with the vegetables. Gently mix (you don't want to smash anything up) the vinegar into the salad with salt and pepper to taste. Refrigerate the salad to cool. Serve chilled with Parmesan cheese on top.

Currant Apricot Rice

T HE SPICES MAKE THIS RICE DISH fragrant and delicious. It's also lovely to look at the anise stars. (Scarlett calls this the twinkle star rice.) This is the perfect side for a cozy winter meal. **LK**

Prep time: 10 minutes
Total time: 35 minutes
Makes: 4 servings

2 ½ cups (625 ml) low-sodium vegetable stock
½ cup (125 ml) wild rice
4 anise stars
½ cup (125 ml) brown basmati rice
½ cup (125 ml) water
1 tsp (5 ml) ground cumin
1 tsp (5 ml) ground turmeric
¼ tsp (1 ml) salt
½ cup (125 ml) dried apricots, sliced
½ cup (125 ml) dried currants
⅓ cup (80 ml) pecans, chopped

In a small saucepan, place 1 cup (250 ml) of the vegetable stock, the wild rice and 2 anise stars and bring to a gentle boil. Cook until the rice has absorbed all the liquid, about 25 minutes.

In another pot bring the remaining 1 ½ cups (375 ml) of vegetable stock, the basmati rice, water, the 2 remaining anise stars, cumin, turmeric and salt to a gentle boil. Cook until the rice is almost tender and the liquid has evaporated by half, about 20 minutes. At this point add the apricot slices and currants. Cook until all the liquid is gone.

Meanwhile, toast the pecans and then set them aside.

Remove both pots from the heat, empty the contents of both into a large serving bowl and mix to combine, remove the stars, then garnish with the pecans. Serve warm.

WHAT'S SO GREAT ABOUT TURMERIC? From the root of the curcuma plant and a major component of curry, turmeric is a powerful anti-inflammatory. Curcumin, the pigment that gives the spice its vibrant yellow color, is an effective antioxidant that protects cells from damage and can also help lower cholesterol. **CM**

Dinner Outside

WHETHER YOU'RE SETTING A TABLE by the water or just throwing open the back door, entertaining in the summer should be easy. We like meals that can be prepped in advance so that firing up the grill is the only thing making you sweat. But with a frosty (and possibly spiked) lemonade on standby, even that shouldn't be a problem. **LK & CM**

MENU
Watermelon Lemonade

Grape Salsa

Gruyère and Herb Turkey Burgers

Chicken and Peach Skewers

Sweet Corn and Green Bean Salad

Watermelon Salad

Watermelon Lemonade

THIS WATERMELON LEMONADE was conjured up during one of Toronto's punishing heat waves. It's light, refreshing and super-juicy. I confess that a shot of vodka may have been known to make its way into a glass. CM

Prep time: 20 minutes

Total time: 20 minutes

Makes: serves a crowd

6 cups (1.5 L) watermelon
    (about ½ of a good-sized watermelon)
1 cup (250 ml) fresh lemon juice
    (about 4 lemons' worth)
2 Tbsp (30 ml) agave nectar (use honey or
    maple syrup if you can't find agave)
3 cups (750 ml) sparkling mineral or soda water

Cut your watermelon into large chunks. Cut all the flesh away from the rind. Pick out as many seeds as you can but don't worry if you miss some.

Working in batches, toss the watermelon pieces into a blender and whiz away. Pour the juice through a fine mesh sieve into a large bowl or pitcher. Every once in a while, run a spatula along the bottom of your sieve to keep the juice flowing. Add the lemon juice and agave syrup and mix really well. Check it for sweetness.

Fill a glass with ice. Pour it three-quarters full with watermelon juice and top up with fizzy water.

Grape Salsa

LIZ AND PAUL, OUR NEIGHBORS at the cottage, spend the summer entertaining scores of relatives and friends. Liz handles the army of mouths to feed with a stable of fresh and simple dishes like this cheery appetizer. We love to eat it all year round, but it's never the same without the sun going down over the water, a glass of wine in my hand, and Liz at my side. LK

Prep time: 20 minutes

Total time: 20 minutes

Makes: serves a crowd

2 ½ cups (625 ml) halved red grapes
1 clove garlic, minced
1 Tbsp (15 ml) extra virgin olive oil
1 tsp (5 ml) chopped cilantro

In a large serving bowl, toss the grapes with the garlic, oil and cilantro. Serve at room temperature or cold with corn chips or toasted multigrain pita.

Gruyère and Herb Turkey Burgers

M Y FRIEND KARINE has a husband who loves to experiment in the kitchen. He was the one who first turned me on to herbes de Provence, a lovely mix of thyme, rosemary, marjoram, basil and, in the more traditional blends, lavender. I love the flavor boost the mix gives my turkey burgers. Even my husband, who believes beef is the answer to all things delicious, appreciates these grilled gems. LK

Prep time: 10 minutes
Total time: 20 minutes
Makes: 4–6 servings

1 lb (450 g) ground lean turkey meat
¼ cup (60 ml) finely diced onion
¼ cup (60 ml) finely diced gruyère cheese
3 Tbsp (45 ml) herbes de Provence
½ tsp (2 ml) salt

In a large bowl, mix the turkey meat with the onion, cheese, herbes de Provence and salt. Form into 6 patties.

Preheat your grill.

Cook the patties on the grill or in a frying pan over medium heat for about 10 minutes, flipping once, and then cook for another 8 to 10 minutes. Remove from the grill or frying pan when the patties have an internal temperature of 180°F (82°C).

Serve on fresh, whole grain buns with your family's favorite fixings.

Chicken and Peach Skewers

LOVE THE FLAVORS of these skewers—chicken with peach is a winning combination. But the first time I made these, my kids couldn't quite get their heads around them. "There are peaches in dinner?" "Yep." "You cooked peaches with chicken?" "Uh-huh." Then they fell silent as they tucked in and cleaned their plates. CM

Prep time: 20 minutes
Total time: 30 minutes
Makes: 4 servings

8 wooden skewers
1 cup (250 ml) apple cider vinegar
½ cup (125 ml) honey
1 Tbsp (15 ml) vegetable oil
1 sprig fresh rosemary
1 tsp (5 ml) Dijon mustard
Salt and pepper
4 boneless, skinless chicken breasts
1 red onion
3–4 ripe but firm peaches

Soak the wooden skewers in water for at least 30 minutes before you begin cooking.

In a small saucepan, mix the vinegar, honey, oil and rosemary over medium-high heat. Simmer this marinade for about 10 minutes until it reduces by almost half. Turn off the heat and pull out the rosemary sprig. Whisk in the mustard and a pinch of salt and pepper. Set aside.

Cut the chicken breasts into 1 ½-inch (4 cm) chunks. Cut the onion into eighths and peel the layers apart. Pit and quarter the peaches. Alternating chicken, onion and peaches, thread the ingredients onto the skewers. Brush marinade all over the skewered ingredients.

Fire up the barbecue to medium heat. Oil the grill very well so nothing gets stuck.

Place the skewers on the grill for 5 minutes. Use tongs to turn them over and cook for 5 more minutes on the other side. Cut into a piece of chicken just to be sure it is cooked through.

Sweet Corn and Green Bean Salad

T HIS SALAD WAS INSPIRED by the abundance of fresh ingredients available during the summer. Please meet the recipe that has been the fate of countless ears of our local corn. LK

Prep time: 10 minutes
Total time: 15 minutes
Makes: 6–8 servings

¼ cup (60 ml) olive oil

3 Tbsp (45 ml) rice wine vinegar

Salt and pepper

4 ears of corn, grilled

1 lb (450 g) green beans, blanched
    and cooled

1 red bell pepper, diced

½ red onion, thinly sliced

¼ cup (60 ml) crumbled feta cheese,
    plus more for sprinkling

Prepare a vinaigrette by whisking together the oil and vinegar with salt and pepper. Set aside.

Cut the corn kernels from the cob and chill for about 20 minutes. In the meantime, place the beans, bell pepper, red onion and feta in a large bowl. Add the corn, and drizzle with vinaigrette and toss to mix well. Sprinkle a bit more feta overtop and serve..

Watermelon Salad

FIRST HAD THIS AMAZING salad at the barbecue that Ben's parents had for us the day after our wedding. At first glance, it's a classic Greek salad, but using watermelon instead of tomatoes makes it so unusual and so, so good. CM

Prep time: 15 minutes
Total time: 15 minutes
Makes: 6 servings

3 cups (750 ml) watermelon
    (about ¼ of a good-sized melon)
1 ½ cups (375 ml) feta cheese or ricotta salata
½ small red onion, finely chopped
⅓ cup (80 ml) black olives, pitted and chopped
Small handful of fresh herbs (mint is great but you
    can use parsley, basil or oregano), chopped
½ cup (125 ml) olive oil
¼ cup (60 ml) fresh lemon juice
1 tsp (5 ml) Dijon mustard
½ tsp (2 ml) sesame oil
Salt and pepper

Carve up your watermelon and cut the flesh into cubes about 2 inches (5 cm) square. Cut the feta into about 1-inch (2.5 cm) cubes.

In a large serving bowl, gently mix the watermelon with the cheese, onion, olives and herbs. In a small bowl, whisk together the olive oil, lemon juice, mustard, sesame oil and salt and pepper. Pour this vinaigrette over the salad and gently toss again. Serve!

Baby Cakes

Blackberry Apple Crostata

Blueberry Peach Crumble

Lemon Pudding Cake

Rosalia's Grain Pie

Mini Pumpkin Cheesecakes with Almond Crust

Chocolate Zucchini Brownies

desserts

Cherry Chocolate Mousse Cake

Cherry and Blackberry Granita

Banana Blueberry Swirls

Lemon Mint Popsicles

Peach-sicles

Pineapple Raspberry Rockets

Baby Cakes

THESE NOT-SO-SWEET little cupcakes made their debut at Julian's first birthday celebration. I wish I could tell you it was baby's first sugar. Alas, as the second child, he experienced all sorts of the so-bad-they're-good things we kept away from Esme when she was a baby. Still, familiarity did nothing to diminish the pleasure Julian found in these super-moist little cakes. And most important, we were able to get the oh-so-important photo of him in his first little collared shirt, covered in icing. CM

Prep time: 15 minutes
Total time: 1 hour 10 minutes
Makes: 24 mini cupcakes

Cupcakes
½ cup (125 ml) butter, softened
½ cup (125 ml) granulated sugar
½ cup (125 ml) brown sugar, packed
2 eggs
1 can (14 oz/398 g) pumpkin purée (or
    1 ⅔ cups (185 ml) of homemade
    purée. See page 17.)
1 cup (250 ml) all-purpose flour
1 tsp (5 ml) baking powder
½ tsp (2 ml) baking soda
1 tsp (5 ml) ground cinnamon
¼ tsp (1 ml) ground nutmeg
¼ tsp (1 ml) ground ginger
¼ tsp (1 ml) salt

Icing
1 package (4 oz/110 g) cream cheese,
    softened
¼ cup (60 ml) butter, softened
1 tsp (5 ml) vanilla extract
1 ½ cups (375 ml) confectioners' sugar

Preheat the oven to 350°F (180°C). Lightly grease mini muffin tins or line them with cupcake papers.

For the cupcakes, in a large bowl, mix the butter and both sugars together with an electric mixer until light and creamy. Add the eggs and mix again. Add the pumpkin purée and mix well.

In another bowl, whisk together the flour, baking powder, baking soda, cinnamon, nutmeg, ginger and salt. Add the dry ingredients to the wet and stir until just combined. Spoon into the prepared muffin tins, filling each three-quarters full.

Bake for 25 minutes or until a toothpick inserted in the center comes out clean. Allow to cool for 5 minutes before turning out of the tins to cool completely on a rack.

To make the icing, mix together the cream cheese and butter with an electric mixer until light. Add the vanilla. Gradually add the confectioners' sugar and continue to mix until smooth. Spread a dollop of icing over each cupcake.

Blackberry Apple Crostata

'LL TAKE PIE OVER CAKE ANY DAY—especially a summer day. But I find pastry a bit intimidating and so I used to shy away from pie making. That is, until I learned how easy crostatas are to make. Crostatas are more rustic than traditional pie, so if your pleated crust is a bit ragged it only adds to the crostata's beauty. The combination of apples and blackberries makes this a perfect late-summer dessert. And in my house it's been known to make a decadent breakfast the following morning. What? It's mostly fruit! CM

Prep time: 1 hour
Total time: 2 hours 15 minutes
Makes: 6 servings

Pastry

¾ cup (185 ml) very cold unsalted butter

1 cup (250 ml) all-purpose flour

½ cup (125 ml) whole wheat flour

1½ Tbsp (22 ml) granulated sugar

½ tsp (2 ml) kosher salt

1 Tbsp (15 ml) milk

2 eggs

2 Tbsp (30 ml) turbinado, demerara
   or any large-grain sugar

Filling

2 cups (500 ml) fresh or thawed frozen
   blackberries

2 ¾ cups (685 ml) peeled, cored and sliced
   firm apples, like Granny Smith

⅔ cup (160 ml) sugar

¼ cup (60 ml) cornstarch

6 Tbsp (90 ml) water

For the pastry, place the butter in the freezer 30 minutes before you plan to use it. Life-changing, we promise. In a large bowl, mix together both flours, sugar and salt. Grate the cold butter with a cheese grater. Add the butter bits to the flour and really toss it around so every piece of butter gets covered with flour.

Whisk together the milk and 1 egg and then stir it into the flour mixture. Use your hands to form the dough into a ball. Pat it into a disk, cover completely with plastic wrap and chill in the refrigerator for at least 1 hour.

See overleaf for preparation continued

For the filling, place the fruit and sugar in a heavy-bottomed saucepan over medium heat and gently stir until the sugar dissolves and the fruit begins to kick off some liquid. Allow to cook for 5 minutes, stirring occasionally.

In a small bowl, mix the cornstarch with the water to make a slurry. Add this slurry to the fruit and stir. Allow it to come to a boil (you may need to increase the temperature slightly) and then take the saucepan off the heat. Pour the fruit into a bowl and place in the refrigerator for 30 minutes to cool completely.

Preheat the oven to 400°F (200°C).

Place a piece of parchment paper on your work surface and flour it lightly. Place your pie dough on the parchment and, with a floured rolling pin, roll it out into a 12-inch (30 cm) circle. Whisk the remaining egg and brush it over the entire surface of your dough. You'll have some egg left.

Use a ladle to heap the fruit filling into the center of the dough. You want to have about a 1 ½-inch (4 cm) border around the edges. The filling will spread so you'll have to work quickly. Fold the edges of the dough toward the center—they won't meet—leaving a 5–6 inch (12–15 cm) opening in the center. You'll have to pleat and fold as you go but don't worry about making it perfect, it's meant to be rustic! Brush the border of the dough with egg and sprinkle the large-grain sugar on top. Carefully and quickly transfer the parchment paper onto a baking sheet. Dust off any excess flour from the parchment paper.

Place in the oven on the middle rack and bake for 40 to 45 minutes, until the crust is golden brown. Allow the crostata to cool before serving.

Blueberry Peach Crumble

'M NOT NOSTALGIC BY NATURE but I do miss the adorable language mistakes my kids made as toddlers. It broke my ex–fashion editor's heart when Esme stopped calling her favorite fruit "gabbanas"! Sometimes their errors did more justice to a dish than its actual name. I was once baking up a batch of these lighter-than-most crumbles when Julian sped through the kitchen and stopped to peer into the oven. His face lit up as he exclaimed, "Pie cake!" Perfect, right? And so, pie cake it will always be. CM

Prep time: 15 minutes

Total time: 35 minutes

Makes: 4 small ramekins

1 cup (250 ml) fresh or thawed
    frozen blueberries

1 cup (250 ml) pitted, cubed peaches

2 Tbsp (30 ml) orange juice

3 Tbsp (45 ml) whole wheat flour

3 Tbsp (45 ml) rolled oats

2 Tbsp (30 ml) brown sugar

2 Tbsp (30 ml) canola oil

2 tsp (10 ml) honey

1 tsp (5 ml) ground cinnamon

Preheat the oven to 375°F (190°C).

In a large bowl, toss the blueberries, peaches and orange juice together. Spoon equal portions into four small ramekins. In another bowl, combine the flour, oats, sugar, oil, honey and cinnamon until they come together but are still crumbly. Spoon evenly over the fruit. Place the ramekins on a baking sheet and place on the middle rack in the oven for 15 to 20 minutes, until the fruit is bubbling and the topping is golden and crisp. Allow to cool a bit before serving.

WHAT'S SO GREAT ABOUT CINNAMON? This popular spice makes almost everything taste better but it also lowers your cholesterol and stabilizes blood sugars. Just smelling cinnamon can improve brain function and memory. LK

Lemon Pudding Cake

THIS OLD-FASHIONED RECIPE is easy to make yet creates rather a fancy impression. It's a light sponge cake on top and a creamy, pudding sauce underneath. I've seen chocolate and caramel variations but my kids love this zingy lemon one. If you can find Meyer lemons, grab them! Although not necessary, they're sweeter than regular lemons and improve any lemon-based recipe. CM

Prep time: 15 minutes
Total time: 1 hour
Makes: 6 servings

2 Tbsp (30 ml) butter, softened,
    plus a bit more to prepare the
    ramekin
1 cup (250 ml) sugar
3 eggs, separated
1 Tbsp (15 ml) lemon zest
¼ cup (60 ml) all-purpose flour
¼ tsp (1 ml) salt
1 cup (250 ml) milk
⅔ cup (80 ml) fresh lemon juice
2 Tbsp (30 ml) confectioners' sugar

Preheat the oven to 350°F (180°C). Lightly butter a 1.5-quart (1.4 L) ramekin or soufflé dish.

Set aside 2 Tbsp (30 ml) of the sugar. Take the rest of the sugar and beat it into the butter in a large bowl with an electric mixer until the mixture is grainy but light. Add the egg yolks to the sugar mixture one at a time, mixing well between each addition. Add the lemon zest and mix well. Add the flour and salt and mix well. Now add the milk and lemon juice and give everything one last good mix.

In another large bowl (be sure it's perfectly clean—egg whites don't like any kind of grease!), beat your eggs whites with an electric mixer until they're frothy and beginning to form soft peaks. Sprinkle with the reserved 2 Tbsp (30 ml) of sugar and beat again until they form stiff peaks.

Fold the whites into the lemon mixture. Using a baking spatula, move the batter around the bowl, then gently lift it up and over the whites. Once the batter is uniform in color and texture, stop.

Place the prepared ramekin in a large, high-sided roasting pan. Pour the batter into the ramekin, using the spatula to get it all out of the bowl. Carefully pour water into the roasting pan so that it comes halfway up the ramekin.

Place on the middle rack of the oven for 40 to 45 minutes. Watch closely—you want the cake to be a firm yet soft sponge, and the top to be golden, not brown. Remove the cake from the oven and allow it to cool for at least 10 minutes before shaking the confectioners' sugar through a fine sieve overtop. Use a large spoon to scoop out a portion of the cake into a bowl. Be sure to go right to the bottom of the ramekin for the pudding sauce!

Rosalia's Grain Pie

THIS GRAIN PIE, a common Italian Easter dessert, is another recipe passed down from my father's mother, Rosalia. The original recipe included candied fruits but many moons ago my mom swapped them out for chocolate chips. I realize some traditions are not meant to be broken, but it's all about the chocolate in this moist, cheesey pie, which my mother also made crustless. My dad and I compete to see who can eat more of this. Sadly, I can beat him. **LK**

Prep time: 30 minutes
Total time: 1 hour 30 minutes
Makes: 10 servings

½ cup (125 ml) cooked arborio rice
8 eggs
½ cup (125 ml) granulated sugar
6 cups (1.5 L) ricotta cheese
1 tsp (5 ml) fresh lemon juice
1 tsp (5 ml) vanilla extract
1 tsp (5 ml) ground cinnamon
¾ cup (185 ml) dark chocolate chips

Preheat the oven to 375°F (190°C). Grease a 9- x 13-inch (3.5 L) glass baking dish or 10 small ramekins.

Cook the rice according to the package directions. Set aside to cool.

In a large mixing bowl, beat the eggs with an electric mixer while gradually adding the sugar. Mix in the ricotta, cooled rice, lemon juice, vanilla and cinnamon. Fold in the chocolate chips.

Pour the batter into the prepared baking dish or ramekins leaving about an ¼ inch (0.5 cm) space at the top. Bake in the oven on the middle rack for 1 hour if you're using a baking dish, 25 to 30 minutes if you're using ramekins, or until a toothpick inserted in the center comes out clean.

Allow to cool. You can serve this pie warm, or try it the way we love it—cold from the refrigerator.

Mini Pumpkin Cheesecakes
with Almond Crust

A NEW YORK–STYLE cheesecake has always been my Achilles' heel when it comes to dessert. And as I'm sure you've already surmised, I love pumpkin. So please say hello to my little friend Pumpkin Cheesecake. Instead of a graham cracker crust, I gave it this gluten-free nut crust that, frankly, makes a graham cracker crust seem boring. It was Scarlett's idea to make these cakes mini, and I have to admit— she wasn't wrong. Popping two of these into my mouth doesn't feel nearly as naughty as tucking into one thick slice. LK

Prep time:	30 minutes
Total time:	40 minutes
Makes:	36–48 mini muffins

Crust
1 cup (250 ml) almonds
½ cup (125 ml) pumpkin seeds
2 Tbsp (30 ml) cornstarch
2 Tbsp (30 ml) brown sugar
¼ cup (60 ml) butter, melted
1 Tbsp (15 ml) ground cinnamon
Salt

Filling
1 package (8 oz/225 g) cream cheese
⅔ cup (80 ml) mascarpone cheese
2 Tbsp (30 ml) brown sugar
3 Tbsp (45 ml) maple syrup
½ cup (125 ml) pumpkin purée (see page 17)
1 Tbsp (15 ml) plain yogurt
Salt
1 egg
1 tsp (5 ml) vanilla extract
¼ tsp (1 ml) almond extract
1 tsp (5 ml) ground cinnamon
¼ tsp (1 ml) ground ginger
Ground nutmeg

Preheat the oven to 350°F (180°C). Grease the cups of two mini muffin tins.

For the crust, place the almonds, pumpkin seeds, cornstarch, sugar, melted butter, cinnamon and a pinch of salt into a food processor and process until finely ground. Press about 1 tsp (5 ml) of crust into each muffin cup.

For the filling, beat the cream cheese, mascarpone, sugar and maple syrup with an electric mixer on medium speed until light and fluffy. Beat in the pumpkin purée, yogurt and a pinch of salt, scraping down the bowl frequently. Add the egg, vanilla and almond extracts, cinnamon, ginger and a pinch of nutmeg. Beat until well blended.

Pour the batter over the crust bases, filling each muffin cup two-thirds full. Bake for about 20 minutes, or until the mini cheesecakes are firm.

Chocolate Zucchini Brownies

THESE BROWNIES ARE SO RICH, moist and chocolatey you'd never know there's zucchini in the batter. Do I dare say that the benefits of dark chocolate combined with those of zucchini make these little babies a healthy dessert? Okay. I'm stretching it, but they are healthier than most. LK

Prep time: 20 minutes
Total time: 50 minutes
Makes: 12 brownies

6 oz (170 g) dark chocolate
  (I like to use 70% cocoa solids)
¼ cup (60 ml) butter, room temperature
1 cup (250 ml) brown sugar, packed
2 cups (500 ml) peeled and chopped
  zucchini (1 whole zucchini)
⅓ cup (80 ml) canola oil
1 Tbsp (15 ml) Greek yogurt
3 eggs
2 Tbsp (30 ml) cocoa powder
1 tsp (5 ml) vanilla extract
1 ¼ cups (310 ml) spelt flour
¼ tsp (1 ml) sea salt
1 cup (250 ml) dark chocolate chips

Preheat the oven to 350°F (180°C). Grease an 8-inch (20 cm) square pan with butter or cooking spray and then line it with parchment paper.

Melt the chocolate and butter in a double-boiler (or use a stainless steel bowl placed over a saucepan of simmering water—make sure the water doesn't touch the bottom of the pan), stirring constantly so the chocolate doesn't burn.

Remove from the heat, add the brown sugar and mix to combine.

Place the chopped zucchini, oil and yogurt in a blender and purée.

Add the eggs to the melted chocolate one at a time, stirring to combine after each addition. Sift in the cocoa and add the vanilla. Stir in the flour and salt until combined, then pour in the zucchini purée. Fold in the chocolate chips.

Pour the batter into the prepared baking pan and bake on the center rack for 25 to 30 minutes. The key to killer brownies is for them to be soft and chewy, so keep an eye on them once they hit the 25-minute mark. When a toothpick inserted in the center comes out clean the brownies are done.

Cherry Chocolate Mousse Cake

I F YOU'RE GOING to let them eat cake, then let it be this deliciously over-the-top number. This is definitely not a mix–and-go recipe, but the airy mousse and rich chocolate cake are so worth the indulgence, and the time as well. **LK**

Prep time: 30 minutes

Total time: 1 hour 30 minutes
(plus overnight refrigeration)

Makes: 10 servings

Cherry Mousse

1 jar (26 oz/796 ml) red sour cherries, pitted
(reserve the juice)

2 packages (¼ oz/7.3 ml) unflavored gelatin

1 cup (250 ml) instant dissolving sugar
(aka berry sugar, fruit sugar
or ultrafine sugar)

4 eggs yolks (reserve the whites)

1 ½ cups (375 ml) whipping cream

Chocolate Cake

4 eggs + 4 reserved egg whites

1 ½ cups (375 ml) instant dissolving sugar (aka
berry sugar, fruit sugar or ultrafine sugar)

1 ½ cups (375 ml) good quality cocoa

6 Tbsp (90 ml) unsalted butter

1 ½ cups (375 ml) reserved cherry juice

1 ½ cups (375 ml) self-rising pastry flour

2 tsp (10 ml) baking powder

See overleaf for preparation

To make the cherry mousse, strain the sour cherries, reserving the liquid. Place the cherries in a food processor and pulse until only small chunks remain. Set aside.

Dissolve the gelatin according to the package instructions and then set aside.

In a double-boiler (or use a stainless steel bowl placed over a saucepan of simmering water—make sure the water doesn't touch the bottom of the bowl), whisk the egg yolks and sugar for 3 to 4 minutes until the mixture is creamy and doubled in volume. Remove from the heat and gently stir in the gelatin and cherries until completely combined. Refrigerate and chill for 20 minutes. Do not allow to set. Seriously.

While the egg mixture is chilling, whip the cream into stiff peaks. Once the egg mixture is chilled, gently fold in the whipped cream. Cover the bowl with plastic wrap and place the mousse in the refrigerator and allow to set overnight.

Preheat the oven to 350°F (180°C). Line two 8-inch (20 cm) round cake pans with parchment paper.

To make the cake, in a small bowl, and using a hand mixer, whisk the eggs and reserved whites with the sugar until creamy and frothy. Set aside.

Place the cocoa in a medium-size mixing bowl. In a saucepan, melt the butter with the cherry juice over low heat. Once the butter is melted, pour it over the cocoa and stir until the cocoa has absorbed all the liquid. Add the egg mixture to the cocoa mixture, and mix until well combined and silky. Sift the flour and baking powder into the cocoa mixture and gently stir until completely combined.

Divide the batter between the two cake pans and bake on the center rack of the oven for 20 to 25 minutes or until a toothpick inserted in the center of one cake comes out clean. Allow to cool before removing from the pans.

To assemble the cake, place one cake layer on your favorite cake tray. Spread with half the cherry mousse. Gently top with the second cake layer and then the remaining mousse. Garnish with Bing cherries if desired. Refrigerate until ready to serve.

WHAT'S SO GREAT ABOUT DARK CHOCOLATE? Made from the seeds of the cocoa tree, dark chocolate is an antioxidant powerhouse and is linked with good cardiovascular health. Choose chocolate that is at least 60% cocoa to make the most of its benefits. A little goes a long way—you only need one small square per day. LK

Cherry and Blackberry Granita

You just can't beat a margarita glass full of cool berry brilliance. And all the scraping and hacking that go into preparing a granita make it ideally suited for the involvement of your kids. But granita's best selling point? The sky's the limit when it comes to flavors. This version isn't as easy as throwing some strawberries and raspberries into a blender because you do have to remove the pits from the cherries, but I promise you, the extra work is so worth it. (And, no, Scarlett doesn't generally wear white for this job, but hey, it's for the camera!) LK

Prep time: 10 minutes
Total time: 3 hours 10 minutes
Makes: 6–8 servings

2 cups (500 ml) fresh or frozen
    blackberries
1 ½ cups (375 ml) cherries,
    pitted and sliced
1 cup (250 ml) water
¼ cup (60 ml) granulated sugar
½ cup (125 ml) orange juice
1 tsp (5 ml) orange zest
Fresh mint for garnish

Place the blackberries, cherries, water, sugar and orange juice and zest in a blender and purée. Pour this mixture into a 9- x 9- x 2-inch (23 x 23 x 5 cm) metal baking pan. Place in the freezer for 1 hour then, using a fork, stir to mash up any frozen parts. Cover with aluminum foil and return to the freezer for another 2 hours until firm.

This is the part the kids will love. Scrape down the granita with a fork to make icy shavings. Place in dessert cups or dishes and garnish with mint.

Banana Blueberry Swirl

Lemon Mint

Pineapple
Raspberry Rocket

See overleaf for recipes

Banana Blueberry Swirls

THESE PRETTY POPS are an easy way to use up over-ripe bananas when turning the oven on for banana bread is out of the question! CM

Prep time: 1 hour
Total time: 3 hours
Makes: 12 pops

½ cup (125 ml) water
⅓ cup (80 ml) sugar
3 very ripe bananas
1 cup (250 ml) Greek yogurt
3 Tbsp (45 ml) honey
1 cup (250 ml) blueberries

In a small saucepan over medium heat, bring the water and sugar to a boil, stirring until the sugar has dissolved completely. Remove this simple syrup from the heat and place in the refrigerator to cool for about 1 hour.

In a blender, purée the bananas with the yogurt and honey. Pour this mixture into a pitcher or a bowl with a spout.

Rinse out the blender. Now purée the blueberries and ¼ cup (60 ml) of the simple syrup. Pour the purée through a fine mesh sieve into another pitcher or bowl with a spout.

Fill the popsicle molds about one-third full with the banana purée. Fill the next third with the blueberry purée. Fill the final third with the banana. Use a popsicle stick to swirl the purées.

Place the lid on the mold and insert the popsicle sticks. Freeze for about 2 hours.

Lemon Mint Popsicles

THESE POPS ARE AN ODE to my parents. My mom is a lover of all things lemon, and mint is an herb I associate with my dad, who had a tiny garden that I helped care for as a kid. It's not Graceland, but who doesn't love a good pop? LK

Prep time: 10 minutes
Total time: 3 hours 10 minutes
Makes: 10 pops

2 cups (500 ml) water
6 Tbsp (90 ml) sugar
⅓ cup (80 ml) fresh lemon juice
    (the juice of about 3 lemons)
Zest of 1 lemon
20 mint leaves, chopped finely

In a medium-size saucepan over medium heat, bring the water and sugar to a boil, stirring until the sugar has dissolved completely. Remove the pan from the heat and pour this simple syrup into a medium-size bowl. Add the lemon juice and zest. Allow to cool about 1 hour in the refrigerator.

Strain the liquid through a fine mesh sieve to remove the zest and then mix in the mint. Pour the liquid into popsicle molds and partly freeze until pops are slushy. Insert sticks in the center of each mold and then cover with plastic wrap and freeze for at least another 2 hours.

Peach-sicles

THESE COOL, PEACHY POPS are a much healthier version of the classic cream-sicle. We have allergy issues in our house so we have to cook the peaches, but if you don't and you have very ripe peaches you could skip the cooking step. You could even leave the skins on if they're not too fuzzy! CM

Prep time: 20 minutes
Total time: 2 hours 20 minutes
Makes: 16 pops

4 or 5 large peaches
½ cup (125 ml) whipping cream
¼ cup (60 ml) Greek or plain yogurt

Bring a large pot of water to a boil. Prepare a bowl of ice water.

Wash your peaches, then take a small, sharp knife and make a small X in the top of each. Carefully place the peaches in the boiling water and let them simmer for 3 to 5 minutes. Drain the peaches and immediately submerge them in the ice water. Once the peaches are cool enough to handle, slip the skins off (this should be really easy thanks to the cuts you made). Pit and slice the peaches. You should have about 4 cups (1 L).

Working in batches, purée the peaches in a blender and pour into a large bowl. Add the cream and yogurt and mix to combine well.

Pour the mixture into popsicle molds, leaving a bit of space at the top. Place the lid on top and insert the popsicle sticks or cover them with a tight layer of plastic wrap and insert the popsicle sticks. Freeze until firm, about 2 hours (or about 300 are-they-ready-yets?).

Pineapple Raspberry Rockets

OUR SPIN ON THE CORNER-STORE CLASSIC takes a little more time to make than a basic popsicle but the payoff is summertime heaven! CM

Prep time: 25 minutes
Total time: 2 hours 45 minutes
Makes: 16 pops

½ cup (125 ml) water
⅓ cup (80 ml) sugar
4 cups (1 L) fresh pineapple
    (most of 1 large pineapple)
1 Tbsp (15 ml) fresh lime juice
2 pints (946 ml) fresh or thawed
    frozen raspberries

In a small saucepan over medium heat, bring the water and sugar to a boil, stirring until the sugar has dissolved completely. Remove this simple syrup from the heat and cool in the refrigerator for 1 hour.

Finely dice your pineapple, discarding the tough, inner core. Working in batches, purée the pineapple in a blender. Pour the puréed fruit into a bowl and stir in ¼ cup (60 ml) of simple syrup and the lime juice. Set aside.

Rinse out your blender. Purée your raspberries and pour them through a fine-mesh seive. Stir in ¼ cup (60 ml) of simple syrup.

Spoon 1 Tbsp (15 ml) of the raspberry purée into popsicle molds and place them in the freezer for about 45 minutes. Pull them out and insert a popsicle stick and give the bottom layer a gentle nudge to see if it's firm. Remove the stick. Now spoon in enough pineapple purée to fill the molds three-quarters full. Put the lids on the molds or cover them with a tight layer of plastic wrap and insert the popsicle sticks. Place them back in the freezer for another 45 minutes. Gently remove the lids, or plastic wrap, and spoon a small amount of the raspberry purée overtop the popsicles. Leave a bit of space at the top, as they'll expand. Put them back in the freezer for at least 1 hour to completely firm up.

Acknowledgments

From LK & CM: This book was born on our website where we work mostly alone. In taking the recipes and philosophies of SPC into the world of cookbook publishing, we found ourselves surrounded by an incredible group of creative people.

To the team at Random House of Canada and the division of Appetite, thank you for the leap of faith you took on this project. We are so grateful to Kristin Cochrane for her encouragement, to the brilliant and dishy Robert McCullough for his vision and friendship, to Lindsay Paterson (so tall! so gorgeous!) for keeping us on track, to Scott Richardson for designing the pages of our dreams, to Susan Burns for pulling it all together, to Lesley Cameron and Judy Phillips for their diligent work on our manuscript, to Scott Sellers for helping us share this book with the world, and to Martha Kanya-Forstner for helping us to find our way through the wilds of cookbook creation – we could not have had a more caring or creative guide.

All our gratitude goes to the production team who created the beautiful, delicious images. An essential part of SPC's journey since the beginning, photographer Maya Visnyei's amazing eye, patience and friendship mean so much to us. A million thanks to food stylist and recipe developer Heather Shaw for always knowing the one thing that would make the dish perfect. Thank you to prop stylist Catherine Doherty for bringing the pretty, an eagle eye, plus a wicked sense of humor. Thanks to Louisa Clements and Sidra Syed for their help in the kitchen, on set and all those runs to the grocery store!

Thanks to Victoria Jackman and Vita and Thomas Kuwabara for letting us play in your beautiful kitchen. To Heidi, Andrew, Maude and Ford Pyper, for letting us take over your home, and to Heidi for her commitment to SPC from day one. Also, much appreciation to Amanda Digges, everyone at eluxe.com, especially Joanna Track and Susie Sheffman, Zoë's Bakery Café, John Flicker and Miwa Yamada of Wagamama Cafe, Stacey Boag, as well as Katherine and Alf Zarb.

To the team at Anne McDermid Agency, especially Anne and Chris, thank you for your early enthusiasm and making it all happen.

Thank you to those who have been there from the beginning: Natalee Caple, The Coutts family, Lisa Durbin, Katherine Flemming, Kathy Magilton, to Pablo Mozo, Clarence Kwan and Jonathon Yule from Arcade Agency, our dear friends at Today's Parent Magazine, including Karine Ewart, Leah Rumack, Nadine Silverthorne, Kristy Woudstra and Elana Schachter, and to Erika Jacobs for acting as SPC's unofficial IT support department. And thank you to all the readers of Sweet Potato Chronicles, we love being in your lives.

And, of course, our families. There would be no SPC without you.

From **CM:** Thanks to my parents for sharing all their love, support and recipes, and to my wonderful parents-in-law for their encouragement. And most of all to Ben, Esme and Julian. Thanks for trying a different pancake recipe every weekend, for letting me take just one more picture before you get a taste of anything and for agreeing to share the good, bad and the ugly of our meals together. And for reminding me the most important ingredient in every recipe is love.

From **LK:** To my mom, who has been the greatest example of a mother's unconditional love and support. To my dad, who finds outrageous pride in the tiniest things I do. To my brother Al for his abilities as a sous chef, and uncle Ray for teaching me about togetherness and that you should always have fun in the kitchen, and to the rest of my food-loving family. With appreciation to Brian and Sheila for all their love and support. To Molly who was the heart of my family's kitchen, and to Hector who relished every morsel of food and family. With gratitude to all my friends for their support, including Alexa, Angelina, Janet and Lisa. Finally, to my encouraging, patient and adoring husband, Dan, I love you and the family we have created.

Index